This book will resonate with many w   identity. I love how Carol is so vuln~~erable. She addresses~~ that what makes us beautiful isn't what we're adorned with outwardly but how Christ adorns us inwardly. By sharing her struggle, Carol will help others embrace who they are in Christ and how they can allow their identity in God to shine. Her bravery and courage will be contagious for others to step out and do the same.

~Heather Gillis
Author of *Waiting for Heaven*,
Blogger at www.heathergillis.com

Breaking the Shadows is a spiritual awakening like none other. Carol's story made me cry, laugh, and reevaluate myself and understand the strength in having self-confidence and self-worth. After reading this book, I realize how the Enemy uses my flaws to try to make me feel inadequate. But through Carol's story, I'm inspired with ways to combat those feelings and lies. I love that Carol added Scriptures in each chapter, and the songs really boosted my spirit. I recommend this book to anyone who may be struggling or who knows someone struggling with their self-confidence. This book is real and resonates with me! A must-read!

~Dr. Tanoa Williams
Public Health Educator
Columbia Southern University

Anyone struggling with self-doubt and unmet expectations will be encouraged through Carol's inspiring story as she learns to love herself, love who God created her to be, and love God himself! I appreciate how she uses the Bible to speak truth over herself and her readers. Her songs help to connect these truths even deeper. This book is an autobiography, a devotional, and a behind-the-music songbook all in one!

~Cassandra "Cassie" Gonyer
Science Educator, Brevard Public Schools
Community Advocate, Volusia County

BREAKING
THE
Shadows:

CAROL
CHISOLM

BREAKING
THE
Shadows:

How to Embrace
Your True Self
and
Live in the Light
of God's Glory

REDEMPTION
PRESS

Published by Redemption Press, PO Box 427, Enumclaw, WA 98022.
Toll-Free (844) 2REDEEM (273-3336)

Redemption Press is honored to present this title in partnership with the author. The views expressed or implied in this work are those of the author. Redemption Press provides our imprint seal representing design excellence, creative content, and high-quality production.

The author has tried to recreate events, locales, and conversations from memories of them. In order to maintain their anonymity, in some instances the names of individuals, some identifying characteristics, and some details may have been changed, such as physical properties, occupations, and places of residence.

Scripture quotations marked (NIV) are taken from the Holy Bible, New International Version®, NIV®. Copyright © 1973, 1978, 1984, 2011 by Biblica, Inc.™ Used by permission of Zondervan. All rights reserved worldwide. www.zondervan.com The "NIV" and "New International Version" are trademarks registered in the United States Patent and Trademark Office by Biblica, Inc.™

Scripture quotations marked (NKJV) are taken from the New King James Version®. Copyright © 1982 by Thomas Nelson. Used by permission. All rights reserved.

Scripture quotations marked (KJV) are taken from the King James Version, public domain.

Scripture quotations marked (GW) are taken from GOD'S WORD®. © 1995, 2003, 2013, 2014, 2019, 2020 by God's Word to the Nations Mission Society. Used by permission.

Scripture quotations marked (TPT) are taken from The Passion Translation®. Copyright © 2017, 2018 by Passion & Fire Ministries, Inc. Used by permission. All rights reserved. ThePassionTranslation.com.

Scripture quotations marked (NLT) are taken from the Holy Bible, New Living Translation, copyright ©1996, 2004, 2015 by Tyndale House Foundation. Used by permission of Tyndale House Publishers, Carol Stream, Illinois 60188. All rights reserved.

Scripture quotations marked (AMP) are taken from the Amplified® Bible, Copyright © 2015 by The Lockman Foundation. Used by permission. www.lockman.org

Scripture quotations marked (ESV) are taken from The ESV® Bible (The Holy Bible, English Standard Version®), copyright © 2001 by Crossway, a publishing ministry of Good News Publishers. Used by permission. All rights reserved.

Scripture quotations marked (CSB) are taken from the Christian Standard Bible®, Copyright © 2017 by Holman Bible Publishers. Used by permission. Christian Standard Bible® and CSB® are federally registered trademarks of Holman Bible Publishers.

Scripture quotations marked (MSG) are taken from THE MESSAGE, copyright © 1993, 2002, 2018 by Eugene H. Peterson. Used by permission of NavPress, represented by Tyndale House Publishers. All rights reserved.

Scripture quotations marked (GNT) are taken from the Good News Translation in Today's English Version-Second Edition Copyright © 1992 by American Bible Society. Used by Permission.

ISBN 13: 978-1-64645-306-1 (Paperback)
978-1-64645-308-5 (ePub)
978-1-64645-307-8 (Mobi)

Library of Congress Catalog Card Number: 2022914933

Dedication

To my loving parents, who will forever be in my heart. I am beyond blessed to have you both as my parents. You were God's best for me.

God Gave Me You—The Dedication Song

Verse
When I was just a child I didn't understand
Why I couldn't do the things my friends did
I often thought how different things would be
If only God had given someone else to me
Now I realize I was such a fool
Not to see that God had given me a jewel
Now I thank God He gave me you.

Chorus
God gave me you to chasten when I erred
God gave me you to show His love and care
And to teach me how to walk in holiness
God gave me you now my life is truly blessed
For you taught of a loving Christ
Now unto Him I give my life
I am so blessed to have a mom and dad like you.

Bridge
Now that I'm grown with children of my own
I try to give them the love you gave
So forgive me for doubting you
When Your way I could not see.

Contents

Foreword

I HAVE SHARED A PRECIOUS FRIENDSHIP for over thirty years with the author of this moving memoir. I affectionately call her Chizzy Whizzy, or Chizz for an even shorter, cooler moniker. We met in Büchenbeuren, Germany, just weeks after the fall of the Berlin Wall. I was newly married and had just arrived in country to join my husband, who was stationed at the US Air Force Base nestled in the Hünsruck mountains near the Mosel River. It is a beautiful, peaceful area, but so remote that even many Germans were unfamiliar with its existence. Like us, Carol and her husband and their young son were a military family and members of the church we attended. That was a long time ago, before we moved back to the States and happily ended up pregnant at the same time—she with her daughter and I with my son.

When we met, Chizz and I had so much in common. We connected immediately over our shared identity as good church girls and gospel singers. We were transplanted Baptists who knew at least the first two verses of most of the hymns found in the red hymnals that were tucked in the backs of the pews of our traditional childhood churches. Her daddy was a pastor. Mine was the chairman of the trustee board of our family's church. I was "West Philadelphia born and raised." She was "OOOOk-lahoma where the wind comes sweepin' down the plain!" We became friends, sisters who laughed and cried together, harmonized together for years and years, and always encouraged each other to follow God's path for our own uniquely designed lives.

I remember when Carol first expressed concerns about her hair. We were still living in Germany, maintaining busy lives as young wives and committed members of our church fellowship. She was a working mom. I was a new professor. She started noticing problem areas, thinning places, bald spots. We talked about the troubling experience she had with one stylist who used a harsh chemical on her hair. We kept waiting for the subsequent results to reverse themselves. The problems extended to her skin. Then she noticed dry spots in her scalp and on her face. We talked about potential solutions, perhaps the need to alter her diet, drink more water, get more rest, all of which she did. But the most pressing need at that time was her hair and how to hide the changes to her hair. After all, what young woman isn't concerned about her hair and her appearance? She started wearing weaves and later wigs to hide the patchy places and the changes that were happening to her body.

Hiding. It's a condition that has plagued humanity from our earliest days in the garden of Eden. As soon as Adam and Eve stopped believing God and His words, they found themselves hiding from the truth. Their eyes were opened, and they didn't like what they saw. So they hid. They hid from each other. They hid from their problems. And they tried to hide from God. None of it worked. Since that time, we—as Adam's descendants—have continued to cover up our physical scars, emotional pain, and spiritual flaws. We keep trying to hide from God, from each other, and mostly from ourselves. Carol shows us through both her story and God's Word that hiding simply doesn't work. Not only is it deceitful, it's a waste of time. And it's exhausting. Carol's story encourages us as readers to stop hiding, to come out of the shadows, and to answer the same question God asked Adam and Eve: Where are you?

Breaking the Shadows also offers a pathway to freedom. It demonstrates that freedom takes many forms. The freedom Christ affords the sinner, mired in the mud of bondage to sin's power, brings a new life of peace and joy and eternal salvation. For the one who has been enslaved to systemic oppression, freedom allows for self-possession and self-determination. *Breaking the Shadows* suggests that God's people can experience a freedom that many never achieve, even after receiving their new life in Christ—freedom from others' opinions and expectations. Carol decided to look directly at her physical and emotional struggles, accept God's truth about all of her, and move forward in full assurance of faith. And she allowed the Lord to use all of her gifts and talents to bless her readers. You will love her songs and be inspired by her story.

Breaking the Shadows will help you consider your challenges, disappointments, strengths, and victories. Carol celebrates your unique makeup and encourages you to accept yourself as God's handiwork, with all of your perfect imperfections. Hopefully her courage will coax you out of the shadows of insecurity, self-doubt, distrust, and dissemblance, and into the light of God's glorious future for your life.

Pastor Crystal J. Lucky, ThD, PhD
Sword of the Spirit Church
Lansdowne, Pennsylvania

Professor of English
Associate Dean of Baccalaureate Studies
College of Liberal Arts and Sciences
Villanova University
Villanova, Pennsylvania

Purpose of Breaking the Shadows

I HAVE ALWAYS AVOIDED WRITING. MY college English professor tried to persuade me to major in English, and I emphatically rejected her persuasions. What would I do with an English degree besides become a teacher or a writer, neither of which I desired?

God has quite the sense of humor. He takes what we think is worthless and makes it worthy. Never in a million years did I think I would ever be a schoolteacher or ever write a book. I'm a singer and songwriter, not an author. I didn't think my life was grand enough or that I had a story compelling enough to share. The irony is that I did become a schoolteacher, and now I am a writer.

My book, *Breaking the Shadows*, takes you on my journey through many years of hating my appearance to finally accepting the reality that I have alopecia. I had lived my life paralyzed by fear and embarrassment, but now I choose to live my reality out loud. My narrative is an unapologetic path from bondage to freedom, defeat to victory, and humiliation to honor.

Eighty-five percent of people struggle with low self-esteem. They feel unhappy, unloved, and unwanted. Suffering from these painful feelings leads to a loss of productivity and prevents people from reaching their full potential. If you are someone who wants freedom from the bonds of poor self-identity and low self-esteem and to begin seeing yourself through the eyes of a loving God, this book is for you.

I was motivated to write this book because of my desire to break free from the inner turmoil caused by low self-esteem and my longing to embrace my true identity in the person God created me to be. As a casualty of alopecia, I battled with low self-esteem and self-hatred. The purpose of this book is to inspire and encourage those who suffer with the same emotional challenges. If that's you, I want to help you discover your true self-identity through the eyes of a loving creator and encourage you to walk in freedom and experience all of God's glory. It is my hope that as you read this book, you will be empowered to:

- Accept your flaws and imperfections
- Let go of insecurities caused by perceived flaws and imperfections
- Accept that you are fearfully and wonderfully made by God
- Understand that God doesn't make any mistakes
- Walk in liberty understanding who you are in Christ

The truth of the matter is that I have alopecia, but it doesn't have me. My prayer is that the words in the book and lyrics of the songs minister healing and deliverance to you, so you too can declare that whatever has you bound no longer has possession over God's purpose and plan for you.

Introduction

WELCOME TO THE STORY OF HOW my life got flipped-turned upside down. Wait, wrong story. This story is not about a princess who left the projects of Philadelphia to live in the lap of luxury with her aunt and uncle in Bel-Air. It's a story about a little girl obsessed with a desire for long hair. It's a story of a little girl who would ironically lose a great portion of her own hair to alopecia, an autoimmune disorder that attacks the hair follicles and prevents hair growth. It not only flipped and turned my life upside down, but there were many twists and turns, detours and diversions that caused me to struggle with my identity.

There is a quote that says, "Beauty is in the eye of the beholder." What is beautiful to one person may not be beautiful to another. I contend that it does not matter what the beholder sees about one's beauty. What matters is our perception of our own beauty. You can compliment someone until you are blue in the face, but if they do not see their own beauty, the compliment will fall on deaf ears.

I was a victim of my own reality and a warped perception of beauty. For years I either had an unhealthy obsession with hair or with the desire for long hair. My reality was that people who had short hair were not as beautiful as those with long hair. I agonized over unattainable expectations I placed on myself. What I had was not enough. I was unhappy with my appearance and sought out ways to change it, until alopecia took away my choices and left me with

> **I was a VICTIM of my OWN REALITY and a warped perception of beauty. FOR YEARS I either had an UNHEALTHY OBSESSION with hair or with the desire for long hair.**

no choice. Alopecia robbed me of my hair, stealing a little each day and forcing me to eventually wear weaves and wigs to hide my baldness. The Enemy lies and robs us of our self-worth by causing us to obsess over our perceived imperfections. We must learn to combat the lies of the Enemy with God's truth that we are His masterpiece.

Humans are visual creatures and live in a superficial society that places great value on appearance. The beauty industry has exploded exponentially. Billions of dollars are spent each year on skin care, cosmetics, hair products, and services so we can make ourselves more appealing. Changing our appearance to what we perceive is a picture of beauty has transcended toward invasive transformations. If we are not pleased with the size of our breasts, we invest in implants. If we desire more voluptuous lips, we get injections. Some people are in desperate pursuit of the idea of beauty. The search for the most beautiful hair, the curviest body, the longest lashes, or the smallest waistline leads to the detriment of our self-esteem and loss of self-identity. And yet this outward perfection we are chasing is unattainable. But God takes imperfect people and perfects them on the inside, allowing us to outwardly reflect His glory.

Isn't it funny how we are never satisfied with the hair we are blessed with? This dissatisfaction causes many of us to desire something other than what we possess. People who have curly hair want straight hair. People who have long hair want short hair and vice versa. However, no one wants no hair. That's right. Who wants to be bald? It's certainly not what I wanted, but that lot fell upon me. Yep, the hand dealt to me. That's right . . . BALD. Dictionary.com describes *bald* as "having little or no hair on the scalp. Destitute of natural covering. Unadorned." I have no hair on my head. However you want to look at it, I am hairless, bare, barren, smooth, or plain old bald-headed. BALD.

Society's expectation is that women possess hair. Whether the hair is long or short, the female cranium is expected to be covered. It is part of our womanhood and part of who we are—or who we perceive ourselves to be. So losing a substantial amount of hair leads to a loss of identity and a loss of femininity. For me, I felt unattractive and less of a woman, so I felt the need to overcompensate for the loss. For example, I refused to go outside the house without a full face of makeup. I no longer went to the grocery store in comfy sweatpants, old T-shirts, and beat-up sneakers, instead compelled to take excessive measures for fear someone would notice the hair loss.

Hair is used as a tool to flirt. We flash that winning smile and stare with a seductive eye while playfully coiling our hair around our finger to get another's attention. After we are sure they took the bait, we walk away, but not before glancing back with a flirtatious hair flip. This is femininity at its finest. But when your hairline disappears—or you lose your breasts to cancer or you have a scar on your face or you suffer from any outwardly perceived flaw—you slowly lose confidence in your ability to attract, and you are left feeling worthless.

> ... robs us of our **SELF-WORTH** by causing us to obsess over our **PERCEIVED** imperfections. We must learn to combat the lies of the Enemy with **GOD'S TRUTH** that we are His masterpiece.

Self-image should not be defined by physical attributes. Focusing on physical attributes leads down a dark hole to comparison. Being God-focused is essential in avoiding that comparison trap.

Although it's aesthetically unacceptable for a woman to be bald, 40 percent of women experience hair loss by the age of forty. Despite the extent of negative perceptions surrounding female baldness, it is quite common yet still considered taboo. There is bias surrounding baldness as it relates to gender. When you see a bald man, you don't think twice. You might even think he looks sexy. On the contrary, when you see a bald woman, sexy is not the word that comes to mind; most probably assume she must be suffering from the effects of chemotherapy.

For women, hair is an extension of our identity, and losing it can have a devastating impact on self-image and quality of life. Anything that makes us think poorly of ourselves can change our personality. You may have experienced this. At one time, perhaps you were a lively, social, fun-loving person and the life of the party. The first on the list of invitees. Everyone wanted to be around you because your infectious laugh made them smile. When you walked into the room, your presence commanded the attention of all. Heads immediately turned in your direction.

Now, you no longer feel confident and feminine. You feel like a different person. On the outside, you look fearless and self-assured, but on the inside, you are fearful and unsure. Though still first on the list of invitees, you can't muster up the courage to attend. Everyone still wants to be around you, but you fade into the shadows. Heads still turn when you walk into the room, but you think they are staring with contempt. Gone is that infectious laugh, because it will only draw attention to your condition. No longer are you the social butterfly. You have experienced reversed metamorphosis back to the cocoon phase.

Society's EXPECTATION is that women possess hair. Whether the hair is long or short, the female cranium is expected to be covered. It is part of our womanhood and part of who we are—or who we perceive ourselves to be. So losing a substantial amount of hair leads to a loss of identity and a loss of femininity.

Unfortunately, this not only applies to women who have lost their hair or who have physical issues, but it also describes many who have experienced childhood trauma, causing them to shrink back into the shadows of their lives. The Enemy loves to make us walk in shame and fear of our secrets being exposed, scared that people will find out that we are not what we appear to be. But with confidence in God's Word, we can rise above the fear and shame. He will be a shield against the taunts and insults Satan throws at us.

God is able to see past the layers of superficiality and know the condition of our heart. There is no need for us to pretend we are what we are not. God knows our heart and still chooses to

> In His eyes, WE ARE ALL beautiful. Did He not say we are FEARFULLY and WONDERFULLY made?

include us in His kingdom work. No matter what has transpired in our lives, God will never leave us or forsake us. He will never turn His back on us.

Even in the darkest time of my bald journey, He was with me, encouraging me and cheering for my success. He wants to free us from the dark shadows of our past and bring us into His glorious light. He loves us for who we are and not for how we look. He is not focused on outward appearance. In His eyes, we are all beautiful. Did He not say we are fearfully and wonderfully made? This means He took great care and time in creating each of us with unique characteristics and features—some small, some large, some narrow, some wide, some with hair, some without hair.

For thirty years, I lived in the shadows, afraid to live my truth, afraid to live out God's purpose for my life. There was a time when I couldn't bring myself to say, "I'm bald." Now I thank God that I'm able to say it loud and proud and bring you along on my journey. Dive into my story, and walk with me through the rejection, the tears, the shame, the pain, and the humiliation. Shout with me as God delivers me from the shadows of fear. Sing with me the songs I wrote at the end of each chapter. Rejoice with me as I go from bondage to freedom, defeat to victory, humiliation to honor, and walk in the light of God's glory.

Finally, be strong in the Lord and in his mighty power. Put on the full armor of God, so that you can take your stand against the devil's schemes. For our struggle is not against flesh and blood, but against the rulers, against the authorities, against the powers of this dark world and against the spiritual forces of evil in the heavenly realms. (Ephesians 6:10–12 NIV)

ABOUT THE SONG

You are stronger than you think. The mere fact that you are still holding on is proof of your depth of strength. The Enemy only troubles people who are a threat to his work—that's you! You're strong and courageous, so keep fighting and keep praying. Stand strong in faith and know that you are a warrior.

Warrior

Verse 1

I've had some struggles
Shed lots of tears
I've suffered heartbreaks
Faced many fears
Still I hear God say
Praise anyway
So I'll lift my hands to heaven and proclaim.

Chorus

I am a warrior
Strengthened by faith
I am a warrior
Covered by grace
I will keep fighting
Whatever comes my way.
I am a warrior.

Verse 2

Danger surrounds me
I know God's near
Facing those giants
I will not fear
He's my protector
He covers me
So I'll lift my voice and shout the victory.

Bridge
Words will not break me
Threats will not stop me
I'm fighting through the flames
I will not back down.
I will not retreat
I'm going on in Jesus's name.

CHAPTER I

Hair Obsession

AS A YOUNG GIRL, I WAS OBSESSED with hair. Actually, I was obsessed with having long hair. I perceived that women with long hair were more accepted in society, or at least by the opposite sex. From my observation of movies and television, the girls with long hair got the cute boys. My perception was further etched in my mind when all the boys in the fourth and fifth grades wanted Elise, as I'll call her, to be their girlfriend because—you guessed it—Elise had beautiful, long, thick, black hair. Her pigtails holstered up near the top of her crown and hung past her shoulders. She was the envy of all the short-haired girls in class. Well, maybe not all, but certainly me. Was it because of her long hair or because she was the delight of all the little boys? Whatever the reason, this situation is forever in my memory, imprinted in my psyche, and it started my obsession with wanting long hair.

It wasn't enough that my hair was thick. It was also coarse, or *nappy,* and what I considered short. I wanted length so I could whip it around as I saw those with long hair do. Some girls would whip their hair so much, I thought for sure they would get whiplash. And pity the girl who whipped her hair in my face. You know the ones? While I'm standing in the lunch line minding my own business or sitting at the desk behind her, her hair unexpectedly hits me in my face. Why must they whip it? Were the actions just what was expected of girls with long hair? Some unspoken rule by which they all abide? Was this a way to taunt those of us who didn't have long hair? I was so offended and jealous that I did not have long hair. It took everything in me not to snatch that girl's long hair right out of her head from the root.

Fourth grade was a painful and traumatic time for me. I considered anyone with more hair than me to have long hair. Whether a girl had shoulder-length hair or hair that cascaded down her back, it was still longer than mine. Seemingly every girl in class had long hair.

I hated recess. I felt like Rudolph the red-nosed reindeer who was never allowed to play in any reindeer games—not because of a flawed nose but because of what I perceived to be a flawed image. In my mind, long hair meant you were beautiful. If having long hair meant you were beautiful, then short hair must have meant you were not so beautiful—and no one wanted to play with the ugly girls.

There were times when I had no one to play with. The boys would chase the girls in an exciting game of hide-and-seek. When I would try to join in, I was told I could not play, and they never gave me a reason why. I just assumed in order to play with them you were required to have a certain hair length. There was no need to pull out a measuring stick to see if my hair length met the requirement. Clearly it did not. To add injury to insult, there were times when they invited me to play with them only to find out the next day that I had lost that privilege.

In my dreams, I always had long, flowing ponytails I could twirl like a windmill. I was the pretty girl everyone wanted to play with, the object of beauty and never rejected. Then I'd wake up only to see my hair was still the same length as before.

I never had the pleasure of knowing my maternal grandmother. She died when my mother was eight years old. I only knew her from stories my mom told me. My mother was the youngest of three children, and she remembers her mother having what they use to call *fits*. We now know that my grandmother had epileptic seizures. Because my mother had not started school at that time, she would care for her mother. She recalled fond memories, like combing her mother's hair. My grandmother was half Native American, and I remember my mom describing in detail my grandmother's long, thick, wavy tresses that hung down her back. *What? The long hair gene was in my family, and I didn't get it? Why couldn't I have long hair?* I felt cheated. This fueled my obsession with wanting long hair. Little did I know that years later, long hair would be the least of my concern.

My hair obsession fueled an unhealthy self-image. What is self-image? According to Dictionary.com, self-image is "the idea, conception, or mental image one has of oneself." The image I had of myself reflected that of a petite, skinny, light-skinned girl with long, *shaky* (a termed coined by my daughter when she got her first relaxer) hair that I could flip in somebody's face. Instead, I was a not-so-short, curvy, brown-skinned girl with short, thick, nappy hair—the complete opposite of my mental image.

There are many factors that contributed to the development of my self-image, such as cultural images and the influences of family, friends, and others. Even dolls had long hair. Do you remember the doll whose ponytail would grow when you pulled on it? It was already long, but you could pull it to make it even longer for a different style. If only it were that easy to simply tug at my ponytail for it to grow. Come to think of it, I never had a doll with short hair. That was not society's image of beauty.

When I was a child, there were not many shows on TV that featured African Americans, and in those that did, I don't recall that any of the female characters had long hair. I watched old reruns of *The Little Rascals* with characters like Buckwheat, the character with the nappy and often unkempt hair. This was a less-than-desirable image in my mind. For someone to call you Buckwheat was not a term of endearment. It was quite the insult. In my mind, it meant that your hair was short and nappy.

Kids like to play make-believe. When I played, I always pretended to have long hair, and I was Rapunzel in my make-believe world. I remember how I'd put a towel on my head and pretend it was my long, flowing hair. It did not matter the color, as long as it was long. I would flip and whip that hair just like I had seen others do. I was not going to be outdone.

Too often our self-image is shaped by societal images, which can impact us for many years. Certainly, it did for me. I struggled for many years with a poor self-image, based on something as trivial as the length of my hair. We must view ourselves through the eyes of our heavenly Father and not on the basis of worldly standards. We are His masterpiece (Ephesians 2:10). He is the master craftsman and the divine sculptor who skillfully and meticulously designed every unique part of our being, from the hair on our head to the skin on the soles of our feet. He took great care to wonderfully create us to reflect His glory.

The comparison devil is real, and he speaks one language—the language of lies. Unfortunately, we need no translator to interpret his language. It's universal. Whether we speak English, Spanish, Swahili, or German, his lies transcend language barriers. He starts teaching us his language very early in life, convincing us that we're not good enough because we don't have long hair, we aren't pretty enough because our face is covered with acne, or we're not worthy enough because of the family we were born into.

He is the MASTER CRAFTSMAN and the divine SCULPTOR who SKILLFULLY and METICULOUSLY designed every unique part of our being, from the hair on our head to the skin on the soles of our feet. He took great care to wonderfully create us to REFLECT HIS GLORY.

There is no formal education required to understand his language of lies. When I moved to Germany, my husband enrolled us in a German language course. The course started before I arrived in Germany, so I missed the first few classes. The first night I attended class left me disenchanted. The class had already begun speaking conversational German. No one was speaking English. I was lost and confused.

The teacher asked me a question in German. She had to see that I was new to the class. Didn't she realize she hadn't seen me in class before that night? I glared at her like a deer caught in headlights. She asked the question again.

Confused and embarrassed, I replied defiantly in English, "I don't know what you are saying." Midway through that class session, I hightailed it out of that classroom, walking away with the mind never to return. I felt belittled and defeated. After that experience, I lost the desire to learn to speak German. Other than *danke* (thank you), *bitte* (you're welcome), *guten Morgen* (good morning), and *sprichst du Englisch* (do you speak English), I scoffed at any opportunity to learn more. Since most Germans spoke English, the little bit of the German language I did know was enough to get me through the years I lived there.

How unfortunate that I didn't embrace the opportunity to grow. I would not even allow myself to try to speak the language. There were several occasions when visiting a German establishment that I could have picked up a new word or phrase, but I was so closed-minded. Rejecting the opportunity to learn German was not a good thing, but it is a good thing to reject Satan's language of lies. When we don't reject the lies he hurls at us, we translate and internalize them, believing without questioning their validity. His lie language is subtle and seductive. He baits us with nuggets of truth, just as he did Eve in the garden of Eden. He said to her, "Did God really say, 'You must not eat from any tree in the garden?'" (Genesis 3:1 NIV). When what God really said is, "You are free to eat from any tree in the garden" (Genesis 2:16 NIV). Can you detect the Enemy's language of lies? He dropped a sliver of truth to engage Eve in conversation, arousing her curiosity. Like me in my German class, Eve should have been so befuddled and confused by his half-truth that she quickly ran to the other side of the garden with the mindset never to learn the Enemy's lie language.

God has a language too. It's the *language of truth*. Truth exposes lies and aborts the Enemy's plans. Truth sets us free and covers us with grace. Whenever Satan fast-pitches his lies across the home plate of our thoughts, we must be ready to swing and combat his lies with God's truth. The catcher on the baseball team is the most protected player on the field. He is equipped with a helmet, face shield, chest protector, shin guards, and mitt to protect his entire body while blocking a pitch. The gear absorbs the impact of a pitch so the catcher does not suffer injury. God's language of truth does not leave us vulnerable or exposed to injury. He has provided us with powerful protective gear. We are equipped with the shield of faith, the breastplate of righteousness, the helmet of salvation, and the Word of God to empower us to quench all the fiery lies of the Enemy (Ephesians 6:13–17).

Lie Language	Truth Language
I am ugly.	"Charm is deceitful, and beauty is vain, but a woman who fears the Lord is to be praised" (Proverbs 31:30 ESV).
I am worthless.	"Why, even the hairs of your head are all numbered. Fear not; you are of more value than many sparrows" (Luke 12:7 ESV).
Nobody loves me.	"I have loved you with an everlasting love; therefore I have continued my faithfulness to you" (Jeremiah 31:3 ESV).
I can't change.	"I can do all things through him who strengthens me" (Philippians 4:13 ESV).

We spend countless hours scrolling through social media and agonizing over snapping the best photo with just the right amount of lighting to increase our followers. We stress over that picture-perfect pose so our post receives the most likes. This is how the Enemy lures us into his web of deception. We assume that we are not as pretty as the one who has millions of followers or thousands of likes, but the truth is we don't know the lengths taken to make the photo look picture-perfect. We don't see the tears that may have been shed or the abuse that may have been suffered. Our self-image should not be defined by the number of likes we receive on a post but by the way God views us. Until we stop trying to cover up our imperfections with a social media filter, we cannot fully embrace our true selves. It does not matter if you are skinny, have full lips, have big feet, have freckles, or have short hair. What matters is how God sees you and how you can begin to see yourself through His lens of truth.

It is important that we understand our self-worth and find our value in Christ rather than in outward appearance. Just like the grass, outward beauty will wither and fade away (Isaiah 40:8). We must accept ourselves the way we are and not allow societal views, the opinions of others, and the Enemy's language of lies to warp our identity in Christ. So stand firm in God's language of truth, and believe that you are more than a conqueror in Christ Jesus who loves you.

> Yet in all these things we are more than conquerors and gain an overwhelming victory through Him who loved us [so much that He died for us]. (Romans 8:37 AMP)

ABOUT THE SONG

Because of God's unfailing love, there is no situation in life that can defeat us. The Scripture says, "We are more than conquerors." Not just conquerors—*more*. Sometimes we feel defeated because we do not measure up to others' expectations. God says we have overcome. As you read or listen to this song, remember that God has given us the victory. Be strong and know you are triumphant in Christ Jesus.

Conquerors

Verse 1
Drowning in guilt
Lies from the past
Dragging us down
Our strength won't last
Out of the shadows
His truth arises
Because of His unfailing love.

Chorus
We are more than conquerors
We are more than conquerors
Fight every battle
Win every war
We are triumphant in Christ
We're conquerors, conquerors, conquerors.

Verse 2
Death defeated
Enemy tamed
We've overcome
In the pow'r of His name
From desperation
Hope is awakened
Because of His resurrection.

Bridge
He nailed our sins to the cross
Buried sickness and pain
Raised from the darkness of death
Jesus lives we proclaim, we proclaim.

CHAPTER 2

Magic Mixture or Fabrication

ABRACADABRA. ALAKAZAM. HOCUS POCUS. AS A child, I was fascinated by magic tricks like the rabbit in the hat and the never-ending scarves the magician cleverly pulled out of his coat sleeve. The trick I especially liked was the disappearing woman—she'd step into an empty black box, the magician would spin the box, and the woman would magically disappear. The audience was left confused and amazed. Where did she go? Then the magician would spin the box again, tap it with his magic wand, say the magic words, and the woman would reappear to erupting applause.

Magic shows left me eager to try my own magic. If magic could cause a woman to disappear and reappear, maybe it could work for other things. Maybe my hair would grow if I said the magic words over all the hair growth products in my bathroom cabinet. I had every product imaginable—cholesterol conditioners, hot oil treatments, keratin treatments—all for the purpose of promoting hair growth. (Can these products really work, or are they just cleverly disguised marketing lies of companies to make more money at the expense of our insecurities?)

When I was a young girl, my mom was responsible for the daily maintenance of my hair. She would always try different products to encourage hair growth. She even created her own product by mixing multiple hair greases together and adding a little Glover's Mane, or *dog mane,* as she used to call it. Just in case you are not familiar with Glover's Mane, let me enlighten you. This is one of the worst-smelling products ever on the market. The active ingredient is sulfur, which explains the reason for the awful smell. The rumor is that it is used on dogs who have mange; hence the reference to dog mane. However, I'm not sure about that. I just know it stinks.

To make her magic potion, Mom would scoop all the grease out of each jar into a pot, bring the pot to a simmer, pour in the Glover's Mane, and stir. Afterward, she would pour the mixture into each jar and let it cool to a solid form. Her recipe was quite simple:

1 jar of Sulfur8
1 jar of Bergomot
1 jar of Blue Magic
a little bit of Glover's Mane

I remember going to school after Mom used her concoction on my hair and never wanting to get too close to anyone. I was sure others could smell it. Ironically, I did not have to get close to anyone. They could smell it across the classroom.

I do not remember my mother using any special shampoo for hair growth. I just remember her washing my hair in the kitchen sink. Mom would lay a blanket over the counter for comfort, and I would jump up on the counter and drape my head over the sink. I loved when Mom washed my hair. Her fingers were like those of a skilled masseur. Her soothing strokes on my scalp from the crown to the nape would almost put me to sleep. She would lather my hair with shampoo, rinse, and repeat. Then she would use her special conditioner.

Besides her smelly concoction of hair grease, Mom would condition my hair with a cholesterol conditioner. Not just any old cholesterol conditioner. She never had to go too far to get it. She just went to the refrigerator, opened the carton of eggs, got two eggs from the carton, whipped them vigorously, and massaged them through my hair. I had to sit with a plastic cap on my head—you know, for the egg to set and do what it was supposed to do—usually about ten minutes or until Mom decided it had done the job. I could never figure out exactly what the egg was supposed to do. I wondered if the egg would fry when poured onto my wet, warm hair or if it would scramble once my mom began to knead it. Or was it just supposed to set on my warm hair and become hard-boiled hair? Nevertheless, there was no tingling sensation, no captivating smell, just the soothing hands of my mom as she gently worked that cholesterol magic through my hair strand by strand. Then she rinsed it out with cold water. It had to be cold because cold water would close the pores on your scalp to prevent oil build up. Whatever the reason, it was a drastic change from the shampooing experience.

My mother went to great lengths to care for my hair. Although her hair growth remedies never resulted in the hair length I desired, I cherished the time we spent together. It was our time, just the two of us. We would sing together, which probably encouraged my love for music.

She would tell me stories of her childhood. She grew up in the Jim Crow era where blacks were separated and considered unequal, so you can imagine the kind of stories she told. I especially like the story of how she met my dad. They were childhood sweethearts who met under a pecan tree in Boley, Oklahoma, or as my dad used to say, "out from, out from Boley, Oklahoma." He always said it twice to emphasize that it was actually a location past the town of Boley—out in the country and unable to be located on any map.

In my mind, my mother's beauty was unmatched. She had fair skin, what African Americans call light-skinned, with the most beautiful, almond-shaped, greenish-hazel eyes. (It was hard to determine the color because it changed depending on her mood.)

I remember she told me the most heartbreaking story. When her mother passed away, her father was left with two daughters to raise. His well-meaning sisters offered to help him by taking one of the girls. The decision about which girl to take was made solely on the complexion of their skin. My mother's sister was brown-skinned just like the aunts, and they didn't want my mother because she was "yellow with funny-colored eyes."

I was heartbroken for my mom. How terrible to be rejected by your own relatives. The people whom you expect to love you the most regardless of your appearance. (I commend my grandfather, who would not allow his daughters to be separated.) As a child struggling with my own identity crisis, I would have given anything to have my mother's complexion and eye color instead of being brown-skinned with brown eyes and short, nappy hair. I saw my mother's beauty, but she didn't see it. She allowed the words spoken to her as a child to define her view of herself.

Words are powerful, whether spoken by others or through self-talk. They form our thoughts, shape our reality, and impact what we manifest in our lives. What we believe about ourselves influences how we treat others, and our actions toward them impact what they believe about us. This determines the way others act toward us, which then reinforces our belief about ourselves. It's a vicious cycle that starts with words.

I grew up a PK, better known as the preacher's kid. It usually carries a negative connotation, for it often reflects on the reprehensible behavior of the preacher's kid. You have probably heard the saying, "The preacher's kids are always the worst." I'm not certain that preachers' kids have worse behavior or if their conduct is less desirable than others who may exhibit the same behavior. I heard that phrase all my life, mostly from people in the church. But nothing could have been further from the truth when it came to my siblings and me. Our father would not allow disrespect or disobedience. We could not do what the other kids did, yet we were deemed by others as *the worst*.

If I sat with friends at church who talked and passed notes during the service, I was the one blamed even if I did not engage in that behavior. Why? Because the preacher's kids are always the worst. If there was a disruption in the Sunday school class, it was my fault even if I didn't do anything. Why? Because the preacher's kids are always the worst. Oh, and let's not forget the saying that the preacher's kids need to sit down. I heard this one a lot too because

I am a singer. I was not permitted to freely share the gift God had given me for fear of being accused of wanting to be seen or in front.

There was no issue as long as I sang in the choir and was not given a solo, but the minute I sang a solo or was given the lead part in a song, the disparaging words began. I began to internalize the cruel and hateful words I heard. If they thought I was the worst, I'd just be the worst. If they wanted me to sit down, I just wouldn't sing anymore. The people who I thought should be the most loving and caring made me feel unloved and not cared for. (Church people can sometimes be the polar opposite of what God calls us to be.) To avoid being hurt by their mean words, I began to put up invisible barriers and not allow anyone to get close to me.

This brings me back to my fourth-grade self. My words, or self-talk, that I was not pretty enough or that I was the worst influenced my actions. In reality, I was rather quiet and shied away from talking to others for fear of being hurt by others' mean words. What I thought about myself influenced how I treated my classmates, which impacted their beliefs about me. I treated them like the plague, as if having any contact with them would cause me to drop dead from a virus. I didn't want to let down my barriers and allow them to get close enough to hurt me. They interpreted this that I was mean and didn't want to talk to them. What they believed about me caused them to exclude me from group play, which only reinforced my belief about myself—they didn't want to play with me because I was not pretty enough or worthy enough.

My mother knew the power of words all too well. "The words of the reckless pierce like swords, but the tongue of the wise brings healing" (Proverbs 12:18 NIV). She experienced the razor-sharp, reckless words of her aunts that lacerated her self-worth. She carried that pain for many years until she found healing in the Word of God. She not only shared stories of her childhood with me, but she also shared words of healing with me. Mom encouraged me to see my beauty and self-worth through the Word of God and not allow the words of the reckless to define me. I don't think she really understood that I was one of the reckless ones. My own words and my own self-talk destroyed my self-confidence. I wish I'd believed her healing words over my own self-talk and just accepted myself for who God created me to be.

Mom was not the only one with a magic hair potion. I had one too. I have never told anyone about this. There comes a time when a girl wants to do her own hair because Mom's hairstyles are too babyish. I was about thirteen years old when I started to style my own hair. I heard that if you want your hair to grow, massage Bengay into your scalp. Yes, Bengay—the anti-inflammatory cream used for aches and pains from arthritis and muscle strains and the product I associated with old people.

Kids do the silliest things at the recommendation of our childhood friends. I remember a friend told me if I plucked out all of my eyelashes, they would grow back long and luscious. My eyelashes were short, wild, and curled and touched my eyelids. I thought, *What would it hurt to try? They were just eyelashes, right?* The summer before I started high school, I plucked out every single one of my eyelashes. I looked like an alien. There is something to be said about having eyelashes. One, they protect our eyes from dust particles, and two, you just look really strange without them. Thank God, they grew back before school started, but that was a difficult summer. I must admit, although they did not grow back super long and luscious, they were less wild and curly. When Denise, my trusted friend and neighbor, told me about a hair growth miracle, I didn't hesitate to try it. After all, friends are the end-all, be-all on every subject. Of course, with my obsession to have long hair, I was intrigued. "Neicy," as I affectionately called her, "who told you that using Bengay on your scalp would make your hair grow?"

She said, "Mother Dear." Mother Dear was her granny. Since we didn't have social media and YouTube at that time, Mother Dear was our version of social media. She knew everything. I was a little skeptical, but it had to be true if Mother Dear said it.

"Did you try it?" I asked.

She responded, "Yes. Mother Dear did my hair last night."

Since Neicy had used it and she looked perfectly fine, I would certainly have to try it.

Don't judge me; I know you did some crazy things when you were a kid too. This was one of my crazy moments. Nothing beats a failure but a try, but this was really dumb. With my poor self-image and my desperate desire to have long hair, I would try anything. I didn't even consider the health implications. Could this cause permanent damage to the hair follicles and, instead of promoting hair growth, result in hair loss?

If you have ever tried Bengay, you know that it begins to feel hot and then cold. It was no different on my scalp. It was quite soothing, so I figured it had to be working. Or so I'd hoped. After a few applications, I did not notice any change and stopped this ridiculous notion. Besides, I did not like walking around smelling like an old person.

The pursuit of outward beauty is damaging to identity. Many of us are quick to try the trendiest fashion, the hippest hairstyle, or the newest craze to make ourselves look and feel better. We are bombarded with images of people who we believe have the ideal body, flawless skin, and beautiful hair. They make the picture look perfect, but we don't know what it took to become picture perfect. Maybe that ideal body is the result of an eating disorder or multiple cosmetic surgeries. Perhaps that beautiful hair is actually a wig. But we see the perfect image and desire to be like a fake image rather than be our true selves.

The idea of perfection is unrealistic. Sin distorts reality and causes us to chase after a lie. This is a tactic of the Enemy. In the garden of Eden, Eve chased after perfection. Convinced that she was not good enough the way God created her, she allowed Satan to interject thoughts of worthlessness in her mind. Why did Eve have this feeling of worthlessness when she had nothing or no one to whom to compare herself? She had the best of everything the garden yielded, yet she was dissatisfied. The Enemy told her that

God didn't want the best for her, that God didn't want her to partake of the best food or live her best life. The Enemy lied and said that God knew that if she ate the fruit from the Tree of Knowledge of Good and Evil, she would be like God, her eyes would open, and she would know good and evil (Genesis 3:5).

Be like God? That's a standard of perfection that no one can reach. Satan tried and he failed miserably. This is the reason he was cast out of heaven. He said, "I will ascend to the heavens" (Isaiah 14:13 CSB). Failed. He said, "I will set up my throne above the stars of God" (14:13 CSB). Failed. He said, "I will ascend above the highest clouds" (14:14 CSB). Failed again. He said, "I will make myself like the Most High" (14:14 CSB). Failed, failed, and absolutely failed. Here is the irony. There was no need for Satan to compare himself to God or be dissatisfied with himself. God said he was the seal of perfection, perfect in beauty (Ezekiel 28:12). He was covered with every precious stone imaginable (28:13). He was anointed (28:14). He had the best God offered. He was perfect from the day God created him (28:15), yet it wasn't good enough. Satan chased after his own lie, suffered defeat, and was banished from heaven to eternal darkness. Eve chased his lies and was expelled from the garden. Instead of living her best life and experiencing everything God had to offer, the lies led her to hide in shame.

The Enemy is still a liar. He is incapable of telling the truth and convinces us that we are not good enough, pretty enough, or worthy enough. He lures and entangles us with his lies, causing us to chase after the unattainable—the perfect body, the perfect mate, the perfect life—but perfection is just an illusion. There is none perfect but God (Mark 10:18), yet we strive for perfection based on an imperfect system.

Thank God for His grace and mercy. He does not require what we are incapable of and has made a way for us to be perfected, even though we are imperfect people. Jesus gave us His perfection and we are perfected, or complete, in Him. Let's look at becoming complete instead of being perfect. Complete means to make whole or perfect, which implies that something is broken or unfinished.

Years ago a friend gave me a very beautiful potpourri simmering pot for my birthday. I couldn't wait to try it out and allow the sweet-smelling fragrance to permeate through my house. When I plugged it in, it didn't work. I was going to take it back to the store and exchange it for another one, but my husband, being the electronic technician that he is, said that he could fix it. He gathered his tools, disassembled the pot, and began working. He removed the outer covering of the pot, then he carefully tweaked and soldered the delicate wiring until electric current flowed through the system. Then he wrapped the wires with insulated tape to avoid shock and prevent fires.

I must admit I was impressed with his ability to repair my pot, delighted that he saved me a trip to the store. After he ensured the pot was working properly, he reassembled it. This was the moment my delight turned to dismay. Although the pot was now working properly, it looked like an eighteen-wheeler had run over it, reversed, and run over it again. My once-beautiful simmering pot was hideous, but it worked. It worked, but it was so ugly. Too embarrassed to set it on my table, I tried to disguise it so that you could smell the fragrance but not see the pot. It worked perfectly, but it was imperfect. My husband had taken what was broken and made it work again. It was complete.

We are the beautiful potpourri simmering pot, masterfully created by God and molded in His love but broken on the inside, crushed under the weight of the eighteen-wheeler called life. We believe the lies of the Enemy that tell us we are damaged goods, scarred by fear, depression, anxiety, addiction, sexual assault, abandonment, and insecurities. Desperate for repair, we need a master technician who can skillfully apply His tools of mercy and grace to cut out the festering wounds and make us complete and whole again—not perfect. My repaired simmering pot was not perfect, but it worked. Unlike the simmering pot, we work on the inside and we are beautiful on the outside when the master technician repairs us. We don't look like the heartache we've been through. We are a new creation, and old things are passed away (2 Corinthians 5:17). We no longer have to pretend to be someone we are not while trying to cover up the pain of our past.

God does not want an imitation of who He has created. We must realize that we are much more valuable to Him than a counterfeit. In His perfection, He created each of us unique and different. Even identical twins are different. They have the same genetic blueprint; however, their fingerprints are uniquely distinguishable. God could have made us all the same, with the same color hair, eyes, skin, shape, and height, but where is the beauty in that? He created us and made us for His glory and lavishes us with love. He would "sell off the whole world" and "trade the creation just for you" (Isaiah 43:4 MSG). This is just how precious we are in His eyes. God loves us just the way He designed us, regardless of how we look. There's no need for a magic potion or for us to take drastic measures to change our appearance. We are more than enough. God is not concerned about our outward appearance. He looks at the condition of our heart. Unless there is an overhaul of our inner beauty, altering our outer beauty is useless. Exchange the Enemy's lies for God's amazing grace.

> But God's amazing grace has made me who I am! And his grace to me was not fruitless. In fact, I worked harder than all the rest, yet not in my own strength but God's, for his empowering grace is poured out upon me. (1 Corinthians 15:10 TPT)

ABOUT THE SONG

The grace of God is amazing and beyond comprehension. It is His undeserving favor to save us and to bless us. Many times I've tried to be perfect—the perfect mother, the perfect wife, the perfect employee, the perfect Christian—and I've always missed the mark. God is not asking us to be perfect. He specializes in putting the broken back together again. Let's stop trying to do the impossible and allow God's grace to manifest in our lives.

Simply Amazing

Verse 1

I'm standing in your
Presence, Lord, today
Jesus canceled
Debts I couldn't pay
Your nail-scarred hands
Lifted me from my shame
Cleansed my heart and washed away the stain.

Chorus

Simply amazing, simply amazing
Grace rushed in, relieved my fears
And calmed my troubled soul
Simply amazing, simply amazing
God's grace, simply amazing.

Verse 2

Though I try my best
To give You my all
I'm not perfect
Sometimes I fall
It's not about
The works that I do
Your grace is enough to help me through.

Bridge
Oh—so amazing (2x)
Amazing grace
Oh—so amazing (2x)
Amazing grace.

CHAPTER 3

Good Ole Press and Curl

DO YOU REMEMBER THE DAYS BEFORE the permanent relaxers, otherwise known as hair crack, were introduced to straighten the coiled kinks from your hair and lay that crown flat? Remember how the smell of Blue Magic and burnt hair permeated a smoke-filled room? Or the burn mark left on top of your ear when the hot comb brushed up against it? Those were the good ole days of the press and curl. Nowadays, it is hard to find a hairdresser skilled in this craft. It seems to be a lost art in the wake of permanent relaxers.

My mother made sure I had my hair pressed and curled every two weeks by my dad's sister, Aunt Roxie. She knew how to fry some hair! I liked getting my hair pressed and curled. Although it wasn't long like in my fantasy, it was at least straightened and not kinky.

I have such fond memories of going to my aunt's house as a child, not because I was getting my hair straightened but because of the stories she told. I learned a lot about my family history and how they grew up on a sharecropper's farm, how they suffered racism, and what it was like for a dark-skinned girl in American society both within and outside the African American race. One story she told in particular made quite an impact on me, and I have never forgotten it. It saddened me and further fueled my poor self-image and obsession for long hair.

My aunt attended college in Oklahoma in the late 1940s. Because of Jim Crow laws, blacks could only attend schools with other black students. That was just the norm; however, what troubled me was how she would describe the discord within the black race. African Americans have long been plagued with internal racism, or colorism, which dates all the way back to slavery—the idea that *white is right*, or the lighter your skin complexion, the prettier and more accepted you are to others, both white and black. It can be summed up in this rhyme I heard as a child:

> If you're black, stay back;
> If you're brown, stick around;
> If you're yellow, you're mellow;
> If you're white, you're all right.

Colorism has its roots in slavery. Lighter-skinned slaves received preferential treatment with the opportunity to work in the master's house, while their darker-skinned brothers and sisters labored in the field.

You might ask, what does colorism have to do with my obsession with long hair? Most of the girls I knew who were light skinned had long hair, while most of the girls I knew who were dark-skinned had shorter hair. Of course there were some exceptions, but not enough to change the image etched in my mind. I connected long hair with being light skinned, so I had two negatives invading my self-image. I could not change my skin complexion, although I tried with bleaching creams, but maybe I could change the length of my hair.

My Aunt Roxie did not have a professional salon equipped with all the professional tools. There were no shampoo chairs, styling chairs, or dryer chairs. There was not even a mirror for me to see myself. She didn't need much to do my hair, just a chair at the kitchen table, the stove, and the hot comb, or straightening comb. But what Aunt Roxie's home salon lacked in equipment, she made up for it with her stories.

Before she started, Aunt Roxie had to part my hair into small sections to make the straightening process more manageable. Then she placed the straightening comb on the stove. It was a metal comb with a nonmetal handle for safe gripping. Once the comb was heated, she would carefully maneuver it through each section of my hair from the root to the end, cautiously avoiding my scalp. I sat there stiff as a board, motionless. I didn't want her to burn my scalp or accidentally touch my ear with the comb. I took a deep breath as she removed the hot comb from the stove and held it as she worked it through my hair. When she returned the comb to the stove, it was safe for me to exhale for the moment before repeating the process again and again. She must have noticed my apprehension, so to help me relax, she told me stories.

My aunt told me stories about her college days when she was in a sorority. She beamed with pride when speaking of her sorority and how she built lifelong friendships. It was as if her sorority gave her a sense of self-worth. She was able to identify with other women who looked like her. She even paused for a moment to show me her sorority branding, of which she was quite proud. Her brand was located on her upper thigh. She proudly raised her dress to show off this symbol of sisterhood and devotion to her sorority. My aunt was a brown-skinned woman who, because of the melanin in her skin, was excluded from pledging certain sororities. She said some sororities were only for light-skinned girls with long hair.

My aunt spoke very candidly of the colorism prevalent within the African American race. As a brown-skinned woman with short hair, she did not meet the requirements. She did not fit the mold. Never mind that she was an intelligent woman. She just did not have the right image. In addition to the societal views of beauty as portrayed on the TV, cultural views of beauty within the African American culture joined forces to further lower my self-image. The score is poor self-image, two . . . me, zero.

As a young girl, I was surrounded by black people. My friends were all black. I frequented black-owned stores. The members of my church were all black. I lived on the black side of town, although my neighbors two doors down were the sweetest white couple ever. They had a garden and would share their produce with us. They were unmoved by the mass exit of whites when blacks moved into the neighborhood.

Until the age of nine, I compared myself to black girls because that was my entire world. In 1972 the courts ordered the Oklahoma public school system to develop plans for desegregation. The world as I knew it turned upside down. I was forced to attend a predominantly white school, and to make matters worse, I was the only black girl in my class. Already damaged from colorism, my self-image suffered a punch thrown by racism.

My white classmates stared at me the first day of school as they processed the obvious difference in our skin color. That didn't bother me so much because God loves us all the same, regardless of the color of our skin. I remember singing the song "Jesus Loves the Little Children." I loved the lyrics "Red and yellow, black and white, we are precious in His sight." I wasn't caught up on skin color because the song told me there was no difference to God. However, I was desirous of the length of their hair.

After a visit to Aunt Roxie's, my hair was straight for two weeks, or until it succumbed to the Oklahoma heat and humidity. God forbid if I got caught in the rain. Then it was frizz head again. Of course, there were no water activities for those two weeks. No swimming, and I had better not sweat too much because my fried-to-the-crisp, straightened hair would shrivel up, and the kinky hair would reappear. In that case, there was an emergency visit to my aunt's home salon. Mayday, Mayday!

If Aunt Roxie was not available, I would opt for cornrows or braid extensions. These were always cool alternatives because I could participate in water activities; however, I do not know which was worse—the pain on the nape of my neck from a misguided hot comb or the tightness of the braid contorting my scalp. But my hair would grow when in these protective styles. Unfortunately, it never grew to the length I desired. The long hair that reached down to my mid-back in my daydreams still eluded me.

As I got older, I began experimenting with relaxers, always looking for the next thing that would cause my hair to grow and make my dreams come true. Relaxers brought on a whole new level of pain I had not experienced with press and curl or braids. Of course when applied correctly, there was minimal burning. However, when left on the hair too long, relaxers would cause the scalp to burn. Oh, and don't scratch before applying, or you'd be sorry you did. I wanted my hair to be bone straight, so no doubt I was going to push the limits.

At the time I experimented with relaxers, I was in college and, like most college students, did not have enough money to go to a professional salon. I was broke, so I resorted to over-the-counter relaxers. Sometimes I would apply the product myself, or I would have a friend apply it for me. The application process could not be that difficult, right? Just follow the directions. Either way the results were the same. Well, I did follow the directions, and my hair never came out like the model on the front of the box. I made sure I did not scratch my scalp a day prior to the application. I even did a strand test as instructed, but I never could avoid that burn. The longer the chemical was in my hair, the straighter my hair would be, right? The burn meant it was working, so I endured it as long as I could.

This reminds me of the scene in the movie *Malcolm X* when Shorty, played by Spike Lee, applied the relaxer to Red's hair (a.k.a. Malcolm X), played by Denzel Washington. Shorty meticulously worked that perm throughout the hair, making certain to get that *kitchen,* the hair at the nape, and work out the *naps,* that extra kinky, curly hair. When he was sure that the relaxer had thoroughly straightened the hair, he said, "All right, let's go to the sink." It was time to wash the chemical out before damaging the scalp and burning the hair. Much to their dismay, there was no running water, leaving Red to do the unthinkable and put his head in the toilet to alleviate the burn. I never had to put my head in the toilet, but I definitely understood what he was experiencing. Several times

I ended up with burnt-out edges or scabs on my scalp from the damage caused from leaving the chemical on too long, but this was just part of the process. What's a little pain to be beautiful?

As early as elementary school, I started comparing myself to others. My best friend Patrice had long, beautiful hair, of which I was always envious. She never flaunted her hair or made me feel less pretty. The insecurity was all mine. The comparison demon followed me throughout middle school, high school, and even into college. I felt I never measured up, although I was somewhat intelligent and reasonably talented. There was something lacking that made me feel inferior and that I just was not good enough.

But God says we are good enough. We don't have to conform to social norms or worldly standards. The only standard we should conform to is God's standard. He instructs us to present our bodies as a living sacrifice (Romans 12:1). He didn't say to present the bodies we wish we had as a living sacrifice. We often focus on one thing that we desire to have or to change about ourselves and allow that one thing to define our identity.

In my case, it was the desire for long hair. But comparison hot buttons look different for different people. Some allow comparison to compromise their lifestyles, tempting them to keep up with the Joneses and be led to financial ruin. Others give comparison permission to jeopardize their health by luring them into dangerous eating disorders. Comparison kills. It kills our friendships. It kills our relationships. It eradicates self-esteem, crushes confidence, and destroys self-worth. On the opposite end of the comparison spectrum, it over-inflates self-esteem, over-rates confidence, and over-values self-worth. Whichever extreme, comparison kills.

We live in a me-focused society with an all-eyes-on-me mentality. In Luke 18:9–14, Jesus gives a parable about a Pharisee and a tax collector that explains this comparison paradox. Both men enter the temple to pray. Notice the me-focused prayer of the Pharisee. "God, I thank you that I am not like other people—robbers, evildoers, adulterers" (18:11 NIV). He even goes as far as to compare himself to the tax collector. Clearly he is me-focused. On the contrary, the tax collector does not compare himself to the Pharisee and is God focused. Humbled in His presence, the tax collector simply asks God to have mercy on him. The Pharisee exalts himself, but God exalts and justifies the tax collector. His God-focused mentality allows him to look beyond his failures and flaws and look to the one able to help. God lovingly extends His grace to him.

It is dangerous to live a me-focused life. If we live me-focused lives, we fail to see the blessing in every situation even in seasons of scarcity. Years ago, many church members and friends were blessed with jobs, promotions, houses, and cars, while my household experienced drought. Me-focus caused me to compare myself with others and wallow in self-pity. I resented my husband because, in my opinion, he could not give me what other husbands were giving their wives. I looked at all the things I didn't have instead of focusing on the one who could give me all things that pertain to life and godliness (2 Peter 1:3). Like the Pharisee, I was so preoccupied with myself that I failed to see the goodness of God. God was preparing me for His future plans. I did not understand what He was doing at that time. Now it is clear. I would be different. I just didn't realize how different. I wouldn't have what other people possessed. I didn't realize that would be my hair. It taught me to endure even if I suffer loss. So I changed my me-focus to a God-focus. I found that His grace is more than enough for me to overcome any challenge I face (2 Corinthians 12:9).

Living a God-focused life eliminates the urge to compare ourselves to others and instead focus on the purpose God has for our lives. You have been chosen for a plan for His purpose. It's a road that only you can travel. I realized that I must walk the path God designed for my life. I don't believe that it is His will for me to be bald; however, I do believe He allowed it—just like He allowed Satan to tempt Job (Job 1:8)—and He's working it for my good. I count it a privilege that God trusted me enough to order this path for me. It's a journey that only I can travel, for I know at the end there is glory.

> I will say of the Lord, "He is my refuge and my fortress; My God, in Him I will trust." (Psalms 91:2 NKJV)

ABOUT THE SONG

The only immunity to life's problems is death. Trouble comes into all of our lives, whether young or old. It could be through repossessions, bankruptcies, foreclosures, unemployment, sickness, death, etc. One guarantee is that problems are inevitable, but we can find refuge in God.

The COVID-19 pandemic has affected us all. If we haven't lost a family member, we know someone who has. It has altered life as we know it. I wrote "He Covers Me" to remind us that life's trials will come, but we are safe in the arms of our Savior.

He Covers Me

Verse 1

A hurricane is raging in my life
The winds are blowing in fear and strife
The sky is dark and my strength is gone
I'm finding it hard to carry on.

Pre-Chorus

Jesus is my hiding place
My shelter from the storm.

Chorus

He covers me
Keeps me and protects me from all harm
I have no fear
For He is near
I am safe in His arms
He covers me.

Verse 2

I was sinking then His love lifted me
He spoke the Word and it calmed the sea
Keeps me anchored when I'm overwhelmed
Preserves my life so now I can tell.

Bridge

When floods are threatening
God is my refuge
When waves are crashing
God is my refuge
I'm not afraid
My life is in His hand.

CHAPTER 4

The Nightmare Begins

THERE COMES A TIME IN LIFE when you start to think less about trivial things, like the length of your hair, and start to focus more on the future, like having a career and starting a family. As a child, you were expected to do childish things—talk like a child, think like a child, reason like a child—but when you become an adult, you stop the folly of childhood (1 Corinthians 13:11). Gone were the days of my youth and imagining I would have those Rapunzel-like tresses. I finally accepted this fact and was content with the hair I had. But life has a way of throwing in some unexpected curves.

In 1987, I got married and moved to Europe. My husband was active duty military and had been transferred to Hahn Air Base in Germany. This was where my nightmare began, but I have to give you a few details that preceded my nightmare.

I gave birth to my son two years after being married. Might I add that pregnancy hair is the *best* hair ever, and I enjoyed rocking my thick, silky, and healthy hair, thanks to those prenatal vitamins. When my son was nine months old, I took him to Oklahoma to visit my family. This visit was multi-purposed: I had a minor surgery on my vocal cords to remove polyps, and I made a visit to a hairstylist. I now refer to these two occurrences as the perfect storm. The polyp removal went well. It was an outpatient surgery for which I had to receive general anesthesia. There were no complications—however, I cannot say the same for my visit to the hairstylist.

The stylist was a trusted friend of mine who was a licensed cosmetologist. I asked her to give me a Jheri curl, which was a popular style back in the eighties and nineties. It was a permanent, wavy style that gave the hair a glossy, loose curl look. She started the service of applying the chemical to my hair and using the curling rods. Then I had to wait. I think she had me waiting too long because my scalp was on fire. I alerted her of my burning scalp, and she immediately washed it out and removed the rods. We jokingly talked about the trouble we go through as women to maintain our appearance. This was no exception. I endured the pain, and I got the desired result, or so I thought. Three weeks later . . .

It was a cold day in November when my nightmare began. I had just returned to Germany from my stateside visit. The day began like any normal day. I awakened to my nine-month-old demanding something to drink. As I walked to his room, I ran my fingers through my hair. To my horror, I pulled out a handful of curls. I ran to the mirror to see what was going on. There were no missing plugs of hair, but when I ran my hands through my hair again, the same thing happened. There was more hair in my fingers than what normally sheds on a daily basis.

Within a few weeks, I had developed a bald spot on the top of my head in the shape of a figure eight, along with extensive thinning to the rest of my hair. I was devastated. I really didn't know what was going on. I thought that maybe it was due to the Jheri curl I got while in Oklahoma. I began to think back. Maybe it was a chemical burn resulting from overprocessing, or maybe the perm itself was bad. Maybe the balding was the result of the anesthesia received during surgery on my vocal cords, or maybe it was a combination of both—two critical events emerging from unpredictable factors. Whatever the cause, I was losing my hair, but I never thought it was the onset of alopecia. Afterall, I knew what alopecia looked like. A girl in my church growing up had alopecia universalis (AU), which is the absence of hair on the entire body caused by an autoimmune disorder that attacks the hair follicles. *But that's not me*, I thought.

I don't have alopecia. I still have hair. It just thinned, and the bald spot will grow back.

I remained hopeful for a while, resorting back to Mom's magic concoctions, and I created a few more of my own with little success. There were occasional glimmers of hope when I noticed hair growing in the bald spot and thickening in other areas, only to regress again. I have since come to realize this was the onset of alopecia areata (AA), which usually starts with the unpredictable appearance of bald spots that can later progress to AU. I was in denial, so I never thought to consult a doctor.

Since we were in Germany with limited access to medical specialists on the base, they often referred military dependents to German doctors, which created another problem. Although most of the doctors spoke English, there was still a language barrier. (If only I had taken the time to learn to speak the language.) I really did not think my hair loss was the onset of a permanent condition. I thought it might have been related to stress or postpartum issues. It could have just been an anomaly that would correct itself with a little tender loving care. I could not have been more wrong.

As time went on, my self-esteem and self-confidence plummeted. When I looked in the mirror, I absolutely hated the reflection I saw. The bald spot was conspicuously located on the top of my head. Because all of my hair had thinned, I was unable to create a style that would cover up the bald spot. I was devastated, ashamed, and embarrassed. *How did it come to this?* I would think back to my crown of younger years and give almost anything to have that thick head of hair back. Although it was not the length I had desired, I did not care. At least it was hair.

I was humiliated and began a downward spiral of self-imposed bondage. I had been a faithful member of a church and served in the music ministry. Church consumed my entire life. I attended Bible study on Tuesdays, choir rehearsal on Wednesdays, worship service on Fridays, Christian education on Sunday mornings, and worship services on Sunday mornings and evenings, in addition to daily noonday and evening prayer. I was at church almost every day of the week.

One night, I was just tired and probably in my feelings about something. You know that melancholy feeling when you just don't want to be bothered? You really cannot pinpoint what or why you are feeling a certain way, and all you know is that you just want to be left alone. Well that's how I was feeling that night, so I decided I would forgo service that evening. While resting, I got a call from the pastor's wife with a message from the pastor that I needed to get to church immediately. I explained that I was really tired and my son was asleep. I didn't want to get him out of bed and get him dressed. She urged me further. "It's okay that he stays in his pajamas, but you need to get to church." I further explained that I did not have a ride. My husband had the car, and he was at church. Still persuading, she insisted and said she would send someone for me, so I should be ready. I did not want to be disrespectful. Out of obedience to leadership, I got my son ready and waited patiently for transportation.

The pastor was already preaching when I arrived at church. I sat on the back pew so I would not disrupt the service. I don't recall what the message was. I just remember he began to rebuke me openly before the entire congregation for not coming to church and called me bald-headed, causing heads to turn in my direction and laughter to erupt in the congregation. Now at this time, I still had not experienced total hair loss. I had one very noticeable bald spot on the top of my head and acute thinning, so his insult was unwarranted because I was not completely bald. It was unwarranted no matter what. Nevertheless, it was extremely painful for someone I respected to speak such disparaging words of me, and in the name of religion. I was paralyzed with anger. I wanted to run out of the service, but I couldn't move. I sat there fighting back tears, hoping that the barrage of insults would stop. Finally he was done.

I calmly gathered my belongings and quickly exited the sanctuary, so as to avoid contact with anyone. I did not want their pity.

Still fighting back tears, I just wanted to fade away into obscurity. I got the car keys from my husband and went to the car to wait for him. I sat there numb and unable to speak. Tears began to roll down my cheek, giving way to uncontrollable weeping. *What had I done to be the target of such ridicule disguised as a godly rebuke?* This is the kind of hurt and abuse of power that could cause people to abandon their faith and walk away from church, but I couldn't leave. Though I wanted to run away and never come back, where would I go?

My family was thousands of miles away. There was no FaceTime, no cell phones, no internet. I desperately wanted to speak with my parents to lament, but that would have been too costly. The German phone company operated on a clicker system. The farther the distance to connect the call, the faster the counter clicked, so all I could do was say hello, ask them how they had been, tell them I loved them, and quickly end the call. Otherwise it would have cost me a small fortune to tell them what happened. I was stuck. Trapped. I had no friends outside of the church.

I had become a part of a community that I fully embraced and loved, but this once-supportive community laughed at me when I was insulted. "Defend the weak and the fatherless; uphold the cause of the poor and the oppressed" (Psalms 82:3 NIV). Was I not oppressed? I was the subject of harsh treatment, yet no one defended me. No one spoke out against this injustice. Not only was I scorned, but to add insult to injury, I was alone and sinking deeper into my own private world of shamefulness and despair. There was no escape. There was no one I could talk to. I couldn't even talk to my husband about the situation. I knew he was hurt and angry too, but I didn't want to make matters worse. His instinct to defend me could have resulted in catastrophic consequences.

To speak out against the verbal abuse, we risked being isolated from friends and maybe even excluded from the community we so loved. So I kept quiet and wept silently. This is what the psychologist Paul Gilbert refers to as *fawn* or *fight response*. When we experience shame, our brains trigger a fear response and react in one of two ways. We may blame ourselves for the offensive behavior of others and adopt a subordinate role, or we fight by attacking those who insult us in an attempt to create a protective barrier. Shame leads to fear, and fear causes us to hide or defend. In this situation, I chose to hide and faded into obscurity.

Even though I was hiding my shame from others, God saw me. He saw my tears. He saw my humiliation. He saw my heartache. When we think no one sees our pain, God sees it. When we are suffering in silence, He knows, for "nothing in all creation is hidden from God. Everything is naked and exposed before his eyes" (Hebrews 4:13 NLT). What a wonderful revelation to know that God sees beyond my cover-ups, looks past my disguises, and sees the real me. He was drawing me closer to Him. I couldn't speak to my mother and father. I couldn't confide in my friends. I couldn't talk to my husband, but I found that I could talk to my heavenly Father. Even better, He would talk to me. He invites us to cast all our anxiety on Him because he cares for us (1 Peter 5:7), so that's what I did. I discovered that I did not have to endure the suffering alone, for He bears our burdens. He wrapped me in His unfailing love and comforted me by His Spirit. God cares so deeply for us and will never insult or abuse us. Nobody cares like the Father. No one understands like Jesus. He is the one who feels sympathy for us (Hebrews 4:15).

I wish I could tell you that I never felt the pain again, but that would not be true. Those words hurt deeply and were meant to destroy my soul and crush my spirit. I simply tucked the pain away in the secret compartment of my soul and buried it so deep inside that I never talked about it to anyone. And it was still there. At no time did I ask why or what I had done to warrant such verbal abuse. I wanted to avoid the risk of being further humiliated or rebuked, so I never confronted the pastor, his wife, or other members of the church. I hid the hurt and humiliation deep within, further scarring my self-image. I tried to combat it by arming myself with faith, truth, and righteousness, equipping myself with the Word of

God. I plunged deeper into prayer. I even busied myself with more church work while the pain festered inside. What else could I do? I could not leave the church or my abuser. The alternative of leaving the community to which I had bonded was much more frightful. The thought of it reminded me of my fourth-grade self—the little girl who was abandoned by friends, isolated from classmates, and unwelcomed in the community. I didn't want to feel that pain again, so I exchanged the pain of being ostracized for the pain of humiliation. Although others cause us pain, God seeks to meet us where we are in our pain and comfort us. With this knowledge, we can keep moving through life.

> For we do not have a high priest who is unable to empathize with our weaknesses, but we have one who has been tempted in every way, just as we are—yet he did not sin. Let us then approach God's throne of grace with confidence, so that we may receive mercy and find grace to help us in our time of need. (Hebrews 4:15–16 NIV)

ABOUT THE SONG

At the peak of my depression, there was no one I could talk to. Very few people knew my shame, and I didn't want to burden them with my pain. Could they really understand my struggle anyway? The only place I found solace for my wounded heart was in prayer at the mercy seat of God. Many days I found myself lying prostrate before Him, crying and pouring out my heart. I didn't understand why I had alopecia, but I took refuge in the fact that He knows, cares, and understands my situation better than anyone else. He gives us a standing invitation to join Him in the throne room.

Throne Room

Verse 1
I'm filled with so much pain
Caused by the weight of crippling shame
Your love draws me
Gives me grace in time of need.

Chorus
In the throne room
I call your name
In the throne room
Mercy obtain
My fractured life
Desperate for repair
In the throne room
God's help is there.

Verse 2
The wounds that scarred my heart
No longer keep our worlds apart
Your voice calls me
To a place of perfect peace.

Bridge

At the mercy seat
Jesus rescues me
At the mercy seat
Glory surrounds me.

Outro

In the throne room
God's help is there.

CHAPTER 5

The Era of Braids and Weaves

RATHER THAN SPEAK UP FOR MYSELF and demand an apology, it was just easier to camouflage my shame, so I concealed my flawed appearance with braids and weaves. Still in denial about my hair loss, I never entertained the idea of consulting a doctor. After all, the hair loss was probably just stress related or due to a bad perm and would likely grow back. Not only did I not seek medical attention, but I also refused to visit a hair professional. Other than my Aunt Roxie's home salon, I do not have pleasant memories of professional salons.

I'm sure some of us can relate to the salon experience. It's like a juggling act, only we are the ones being manipulated. You arrive for your appointment to discover you are one of five booked at the same time, so you sit and wait patiently while breathing in smoke fumes from hot curling irons, chemical products, and sometimes burnt hair. In addition to being overbooked with scheduled appointments, walk-ins are welcomed.

While waiting, you can browse through a plethora of magazines, as if this will keep you from intensely watching the clock on the wall. Finally it's your turn, but only for the shampoo. Then your hair has to be conditioned. While you're sitting under the dryer, the stylist can complete the services of a couple of clients whose appointments were prior to yours. The dryer timer expires. You know the stylist heard the timer go off, yet you continue sitting there waiting for your turn. You have time to browse through even more magazines. The stylist finally completes the services for the previous clients, so now it's time to wash the conditioner out of your hair, right? No. She can squeeze in one more shampoo before rinsing out the conditioner and roller setting your hair. So you wait again.

The vicious cycle continues until you have wasted hours in the salon. Well, I had decided I didn't want to be a victim and held hostage. This was not the only reason I didn't go to the hair salon. I was just too embarrassed and ashamed of my appearance. I didn't want anyone to see me. I felt ugly. I looked awful. Hideous. I didn't want to be the object of sneers and jeers or pitiful contempt. In the salon, everyone would see me. I would have to sit openly and completely exposed among women who had hair. Long hair, short hair, black hair, gray hair, curly hair, straight hair—it didn't matter what type of hair they had. They had hair, and mine was gone, slowly nearing extinction.

Rather than be seen among so many women, I would prefer a private session where no one else would be in the salon. You know, like the rich and famous and exclusive clientele, but I knew this luxury would come with a price I could not afford to pay. My only options were to suffer embarrassment or do my own hair. The thought of being humiliated was too overwhelming for me, so I decided that I would style what little hair I had left.

I taught myself how to style hair without the convenience of YouTube videos. I became my own master stylist. Whatever the popular hairstyle was at that time, I learned to copy. Whether braids or weaves, I did it. It was time consuming and even tedious at times, but I had no other choice but to learn or suffer humiliation. So instead of facing my fears, I stretched myself and mastered braiding my own hair, a skill that proved to be quite useful later.

I meticulously parted my hair into equal sections with a fine-toothed comb. I carefully separated the synthetic hair to add length and thickness to what hair I had of my own, making sure that each part was the same size so that one braid would not be larger than another. I wrapped the synthetic hair around a piece of my sectioned hair so there were a total of three strands. Then I began braiding by maneuvering the right section under the middle section and repeating with the left section under the middle. I continued in this manner until I reached the end of the braid. This process went on until my entire head was covered. Now I had enough hair to hide the bald spot. I could swoop all the braids in a style to one side of my head to cover the bald spot, or I could gather them up into a bun. The bald spot was now disguised. Mission accomplished.

The braids were like a bandage covering a gaping wound—a wound that would not heal, for every time I had to redo my hair, the bandage was ripped off. We do the same thing with our mental wounds. We try to cover them up with a beautiful smile while frowning on the inside. We try to hide them behind spirited laughter while inwardly suffering. Scars we carry around for years are buried deep within our psyche. Some scars are so deep we forget they exist. They lie dormant waiting to resurface and waiting to rob us of our confidence and self-worth.

Braiding was not the only weapon in my arsenal of disguises. When my hair was so thin that braided hairstyles would no longer cover the bald spots, I resorted to weaves. Weaved coifs were great. There was no need to upsweep hair to cover the imperfections. It provided full coverage. There was no chance of exposing my secret. I could wear it as long or as short as I wanted to. Of course, I chose the long styles, so I could finally have *shaky* hair. I could now do what I envied and what angered me as a child. I could flip my hair in the faces of others if I wanted, but of course, I did not.

I owned my long, weaved hair. Now I could be the envy of others. I wore it as if it were my own natural hair. When asked, "Is that your hair?" I would respond with a resounding, "Yes." Since I had purchased the hair, technically it was mine.

I noticed I had a different mindset when I had long hair. As Patti Labelle sang, "I got a new attitude." I was "feeling good from my head to my shoes." As my mother used to say, "she's feeling herself." I no longer had to be ashamed and embarrassed. I could walk with my head held high. I perceived that when people looked at me, they no longer pitied the young lady with thinning hair and bald spots, wondering what terminal illness I was suffering from. They saw someone who was beautiful and desirable. Someone whom they could welcome into the inner circle of friends. Someone who added value to the group. No longer would I be the little girl playing by herself on the playground. I became a part of the in crowd. What I failed to realize was that I was slipping into a spirit of pridefulness.

In an essay by Jonathan Edwards, he states that pride, by nature, is secret and not easy to detect and is best identified by its effects. One of those effects is superficiality. I had been infected by pride. It was so subtle, but it had encompassed my heart and was concealed under a layer of pretense. I took great pleasure in adorning long hair that was not even my own. Instead of coming to terms with the reality that I was going bald, I chose to live a lie, and that lie bred pride. Just like comparison, pride kills too. It prevents us from seeing the real problem and asking for help.

I pretended to be who I wanted to be while covering my insecurities and hiding my baldness. What I had so cleverly disguised from man was totally exposed before God. What I masqueraded on the outside, God saw right through. He looked beyond my outward appearance and even looked beyond my prideful heart. He saw the real me, the inner me—the one that was wounded, injured, and abused. I had forgotten what was important and what God valued most. He doesn't care about the way we fix our hair, the jewelry we wear, or the clothes we wear. That's what man values, but God values the unfading beauty of our true inner self—the "beauty of a gentle and quiet spirit" (1 Peter 3:3–4 GNT). This is most valued in God's sight. I took my eyes off my true value and focused on the outward that perishes daily (2 Corinthians 4:16). My prideful heart was exposed and open before Him (Hebrews 4:13), but still I was not ready to accept my new truth and the reality that I was going bald.

Several years passed before I fully embraced my truth, yet God is so merciful. He never required of me more than what I was able. It wasn't time for me to uncover my baldness. God's timing is perfect, and His ways are far above our ways (Isaiah 55:8). He is sovereign and moves when and how He wants. Had I exposed my true self before God's timing, it would have destroyed me. I lacked courage. My faith was weak.

No matter what we go through, God has a plan for our lives. He called us before we were born and even knew our names (Isaiah 49:1). I know reaching beyond our pain or seeing past our struggles is near impossible, but trust God. He knows our future and wants us to prosper. Many times I questioned God. *Why me?* I cried countless tears on my pillow, spent sleepless nights pacing the floor, and lashed out in anger because I didn't understand God's plan. Like clay in the hands of a gifted potter, everything that we experience is to shape and mold us for His glory.

Instead of asking, "Why me?" I've learned to ask, "Why not me?" God uses imperfect people to complete His perfect plan. Abraham was a talebearer who became the father of faith. Sarah was a doubter who later gave birth well past the age of childbearing. Jacob was conniving until he wrestled with God, and his name was changed to Israel. Moses was a stutterer, but God used him to deliver His people from bondage. The woman at the well was promiscuous, but she became a great evangelist. Peter cussed, but later preached on the day of Pentecost and converted three thousand souls to Christ. Paul endorsed death sentences for many, but this didn't stop him from writing most of the New Testament.

They all have something in common; like us, they were broken yet called, flawed yet chosen. In spite of our failures, hang-ups, shortcomings, appearances, etc., we are treasures, and God wants to use us to build His kingdom. So the answer to the question, "Why me?" is emphatically a resounding, "For His glory." Paul says, "For I consider [from the standpoint of faith] that the sufferings of the present life are not worthy to be compared with the glory that is about to be revealed to us *and* in us" (Romans 8:18 AMP). I know it doesn't feel like it right now, but the present suffering is for His glory.

The sickness in our body is for His glory. The battle in our mind is for His glory. The struggle in our marriage is for His glory. The difficulty of our job is for His glory. The attack against our children is for His glory. God has a plan. Trust that He knows how to stop the pain and turn our sorrow to joy and our defeat to victory. I once walked in the shadows of fear, but now I am living in the light of God's glory. You can too. Trust Him.

> Be still, and know that I am God: I will be exalted among the heathen, I will be exalted in the earth. (Psalms 46:10 KJV)

ABOUT THE SONG

One afternoon I received a phone call from my best friend, Marlene. She asked me to pray for our niece who had carried her second child to almost full-term. (Since we've been best friends for over thirty years, I feel like her family is mine, so her niece is my niece.) She began hemorrhaging a few weeks before her due date, and the doctors feared that she was losing the baby. We prayed while on the phone. I prayed again when we got off the phone. Needless to say, the doctor's fear became our nightmare. Our niece lost the baby. When I got the news, I began to cry and hum the melody to this song. God had downloaded the lyrics in my spirit. I don't know why bad things happen to us, but I do believe that God is in control. So whatever it is that you are facing today, be still and trust God.

Be Still

Verse 1

I won't question why
Things happen like they do
One minute there is joy
The next there comes bad news
Knocks me to my knees
Causes me to grieve
I don't understand, Lord please take my hand.

Chorus

Be still and know
That He is God
His sovereign will
I want no matter what
He knows the way
And what is best
So be still and know that He is God
Just be still and know that He is God.

Verse 2

Didn't think that I
Could face another day
But God, You are my strength
You take the pain away
When my hope is gone
By faith I'll carry on
From sorrow to joy
My hope evermore.

Bridge

He can move a mountain
He can calm the sea
He can speak to the wind
He can take care of me.

CHAPTER 6
Wigging Me Out

ABOUT FOURTEEN YEARS AFTER MY HAIR began falling out, I finally realized it was not going to grow back, but it was just easier to continue the cover-up rather than allow people to see the real me. I could try all the cover-up styles in the world, but the reality was that my hair loss was progressing. It advanced to the point where I was totally bald on the top and sides of my head. Even Bozo the Clown had more hair than I did. I could no longer camouflage with braids or disguise with weaves. I had no other option but to resort to wearing wigs. During the time I had worn braids and weaves, I walked in denial and would not accept the fact that I was losing more and more hair every day. Finally conceding to the reality of my baldness brought feelings of fear and loneliness.

A wig? I now had to wear one. Fortyish was far too young to have to wear a wig. There were no more options. I had no other choice. I feared that by wearing a wig I would appear older than I was. The only people who wore wigs were the older mothers in the church, and their wigs looked like wigs. Some looked as if they had been around since the turn of the century. They lacked shine, and in some cases, they looked as if rats had made a meal out of them, chewing and gnawing the threads. I don't think the church mothers were covering up bald heads under those wigs. I think it was just easier for them to manage. If only that were the case for me. Not only was I hiding a bald head, I was covering up my shame, all the while fearful of being exposed.

My first experience wig shopping was demoralizing. I didn't want anyone to go with me for moral support because that meant I would have to tell them why I was going shopping for a wig. This was my secret shame that I didn't want anyone else to know. I was alone and afraid, reluctant to go to the wig store. It was as if I were conceding defeat, but I was defeated. Baldness had won, conquering my already damaged self-image and self-esteem. I pulled up to the parking lot of the wig store. It seemed so surreal.

This can't be happening. I sat there with tears streaming down my face, sobbing uncontrollably. I tried to pull myself together and muster the courage to accomplish the task before me. After about fifteen minutes, I opened the car door and stepped out onto the pavement. It was one of the hardest steps of my life. Making steps meant progress, but I didn't want to progress to wearing wigs. Each step brought me closer to the door of the wig store and closer to my truth. I walked in and began to browse through the shelves of wigs. There was every wig imaginable on display. There were long ones, short ones, brown ones, black ones, blond ones, human hair, synthetic hair. The number of choices was daunting. I must have looked rather overwhelmed because the store owner asked, "Are you okay?" with a look of concern on her face. She could tell that I'd been crying.

I said, "Yes, I'm okay. I just have to find a wig, and there are so many to choose from."

She offered her assistance and asked, "Is there a grand occasion or special event?" Oh, how I wished that was the case.

"No," I responded. I understood that she was trying to narrow my choices, but I didn't want to tell her why I needed a wig.

She said, "What style and what color are you looking for?"

I really hadn't thought about any of these questions. I just knew I needed a wig to cover up my shame.

She proceeded to choose a few selections for me to try on. She placed the wigs on a vanity table in front of a mirror and said, "Here have a seat so we can try them on."

Although the table was in a less populated area of the store, it was not secluded. Other wig shoppers would be able to see me try on wigs. I reluctantly sat in the chair staring intensely at those wigs resting on Styrofoam heads with their plastic facial features. It was as if they were staring back at me with contempt, mocking and laughing at me. Who were they to mock me? After all, they didn't have bodies or anything else. That didn't stop their thundering, ridiculing voices in my head. I reached out to touch one of the wigs in an attempt to silence their taunts. It felt stiff, unlike my own hair. I don't know why I expected anything different. It was not my hair. It was synthetic, plastic-heated and strewn together to mimic hair. I felt pathetic that I had to resort to wearing plastic on my head.

"Okay," the store owner said, "Let's take your hat off so we can try these on."

Still not wanting to reveal my secret, I asked, my voice quivering, "Do you have a private room where I can try these on?"

She sensed my anxiety and apprehension and asked, "What's wrong?"

I began to cry, whispering, "I'm bald." There, I said it. "I'm bald."

It seemed those talking wig heads gasped in horror at my declaration. I didn't want to say it. It was if saying it aloud would make it true. Well, it was already true. It was my reality. There was no hiding from it any longer. I must admit it was easier to reveal my secret to her than it was to others. It was probably the fact that she was a complete stranger and I might never see her again.

She didn't look surprised when I disclosed my truth to her. I expected her to gasp in disgust, but she appeared unfazed by the news. She just gently grabbed my hand and escorted me to a small storeroom. "Several of my customers are bald, so you are not alone. I've seen it before, so there's no need to fear. This is a no-judgment zone," she said, speaking softly with such comforting words that put me at ease.

I felt less apprehensive about taking off my hat to try on the wigs she'd selected for me.

"Okay, honey, let's try this one first." She gently removed the wig from the Styrofoam head. It was a sassy little mixed-color, wavy bob. She slowly placed the wig on my head and said, "This one is very pretty. It's going to look great on you." My mouth gaped open with a look of panic on my face. It was a hot, tangled mess. Clearly, she didn't see what I saw on my head, but she did see the dreadful look on my face and urged me, "Close your eyes."

I gladly complied with her command because I looked awful.

She began to manipulate the wig with a brush and ran her fingers through it one wave at a time. No amount of brushing was going to make this wig look good. When she told me to open my eyes, I squinted through one eye, trying to brace myself for what I would see. *Hmmm, not too bad.* I squinted through the other eye. Finally, both eyes popped open in surprise. The transformation was unbelievable. The mop she initially placed on my head had morphed into a thing of beauty.

"You like?" she asked.

The waves careened ever so slightly along my hairline and rested just above my shoulders, framing my high cheekbones just right. It was lovely, even life giving. "I love it."

What started as a dreadful experience turned out to be a confidence booster. My entire perspective on wigs changed. If I had to wear wigs, I could at least be cute and stylish, unlike the old church mothers of yesteryear. I left the wig store a different person, high-spirited and cheerful, not the dejected bald woman who had entered the store. Though I was hopeful, I still shook in fear underneath that wig.

The fear of wearing a wig seemed insurmountable, and the shame was debilitating. I felt helpless and vulnerable. *What if I lose my wig in a gust of high wind?* Well, I did almost lose my wig in a gust of wind. Friends were visiting, and as was customary, we would walk our guests to their car as part of our farewell ritual. Often we would strike up another conversation before they got in their car, which was the case on this particular day. Because it was windy, I knew I had to hold my wig down. The moment I moved my hand off the top of my head, I began to feel my wig lifting. I was horrified at what might have happened if my daughter wasn't there. Her quick response saved me further embarrassment. She grabbed my wig, so it wasn't completely swept off my head, giving new meaning to *gone with the wind,* and tumbling down the street like a tumbleweed. I always wore at least one wig cap underneath my wig, so if it fell off, my bald head would not be exposed. However, most times I wore two wig caps to make sure if exposed no one would see my hairless head. Still, the very thought of my wig blowing off terrified me. Even though these friends knew I wore wigs, it was still humiliating. It caused an uproar of laughter. I had to laugh to keep from crying.

I dreaded putting on my wig every day for work. At that time, I was a middle school teacher, and the very thought of losing my wig while in front of a classroom full of twelve- and thirteen-year-old students paralyzed me with fear. Kids at this age can be merciless. *What would I do if one of them attempted to snatch off my wig?* I replayed all the likely scenarios in my mind over and over again. I could do nothing and laugh about it, because certainly they would. I could run out of the room. I could stay in the room and cry. I could fight back, which was never an option if I wanted to keep my job. I wasn't prepared for what actually happened.

One day while I was teaching, students raised their hands to ask questions about the lesson. I was excited because that meant they were at least engaged in the topic, unlike some days when they would just stare at me like a deer caught in headlights. They kept raising their hands, one after another. Some even gave examples of their own experiences. These are the moments teachers live for. I was elated until . . . there's always one.

This particular student rarely said anything in class, if he even showed up, so for him to raise his hand meant I must have really reached him that day—or so I thought. He waited patiently until I called his name. "Mrs. Chisolm," he said, "is that a wig?"

You know that feeling you get in your stomach when the roller-coaster ride plummets from the apex at a high rate of speed? You're sitting there anticipating the drop, when suddenly it plunges down the track, propelling you into a loop that leaves you hanging upside down. Just when your stomach repositions itself, you are thrust into another loop, resulting in the violent release of your stomach content. Well, that was how I felt. My stomach knotted. My heart sank. I began to sweat. It felt as though time had frozen, and I was suspended in that moment.

I experienced an emotional rollercoaster, rounding those curves and looping upside down, inwardly screaming while outwardly trying to keep it all together. It was the moment I had always feared. Just when things were going so well.

The other students were interested in learning more, and their curiosity peaked. Not only did this student disrupt the learning environment, but he also humiliated me in front of the entire class in the process. Some students laughed. Others chimed in wanting to know if I was wearing a wig. A few others, embarrassed for me, just sat bewildered. What was I going to do? All the scenarios I had replayed so many times before flooded my mind. Pick one. I wanted to cry, but that would show vulnerability, and you can't do that with middle schoolers. They would push that button the remainder of the school year. I wanted to leave the room, but I couldn't leave students to attend to their own folly. I wanted to yell at him, but that would not have been professional. I wanted to put him out of the classroom, but how could I justify putting him out when all he did was ask a question? I did the only thing I could do. I ignored him and continued the instruction.

I thought avoiding the student's question was a brilliant tactical diversion. My strategy to redirect all the students' attention back to the lesson was a masterful maneuver. I could not have been more wrong.

He asked again, "Is that a wig?"

I stood in front of the class, unable to move. You could hear a pin drop as they silently waited for my response, their eyes fixed on me. I said nothing, hoping the bell would ring to avert my response, but it didn't.

He added his opinion that no one asked for. "It looks like a wig to me."

This could not be happening. I had thought the worst of it was over, but his comment catapulted me into the second loop of my emotional roller-coaster ride. I lost total control of the situation. Thank God, I didn't lose the content of my stomach.

Students were laughing and chatting among themselves, whispering to one another. Those who were once embarrassed for me succumbed to the pressure of joining the rest of the class. The allies I once had jumped ship.

I was devastated. *What will I do now? Think quick, Carol. You've got to come up with another plan.* Just then the bell rang to change classes. I was saved by the bell, literally, but the damage to my soul and my self-image had been done. I had managed to make it through that ordeal outwardly showing no weakness, but inside I was crushed. Thank God the following period was my lunch break because I wasn't going to make it through another class period without an emotional breakdown.

As the students left the classroom one by one, I stood at the door smiling on the outside but broken on the inside. "Have a great day, guys," I said, fighting back tears. It seemed like it took forever for the students to leave the classroom that day. One student left his book in the classroom and had to go back inside to get it. "Hurry, you're going to be late," I said. Actually I wanted him to hurry up and leave before my meltdown.

I sat at my desk and wept bitterly, unable to eat lunch and unable to prepare lesson plans. All I could do was cry. I hated it.

Hated my life. Hated the way I looked with a wig and without. It would be different if the wig were just another accessory like my earrings, but it was not. It was an absolute necessity to which I felt enslaved. I felt hopeless and helpless. I could not tell my colleagues about the situation. Perhaps they did not realize I was wearing a wig, and to tell them meant I had to reveal my secrets.

The Enemy of our soul wants to embarrass and humiliate us. He takes great pleasure in crushing our spirits and destroying our self-esteem, but God is the lifter of our heads (Psalm 3:3). As I sat there at my desk, demoralized and discouraged, I wanted nothing more than to crawl under my desk in an attempt to escape the pain, but that wouldn't work. My students depended on me to provide an environment conducive for learning. *Pull yourself together, girl.* At that moment, I turned to my bookshelf. I had forgotten about the compact devotional I had tucked away for those days when I needed some encouragement—when I felt overwhelmed from pouring into students who sometimes were complacent, indifferent, and uninterested. I wiped my tears as I reached for the book. Flipping through the pages, I turned to the devotional on Psalm 18:

> I will love thee, O Lord, my strength. The Lord is my rock, and my fortress, and my deliverer; my God, my strength, in whom I will trust; my buckler, and the horn of my salvation, and my high tower. I will call upon the Lord, who is worthy to be praised: so shall I be saved from mine enemies. (Psalm 18:1–3 KJV)

I started to cry again, but this time they were tears of joy. It was as if God spoke directly to me. He swooped down and wrapped me in a blanket of His grace. As I read through the passage several times, I began to recite over and over, "God, you are my buckler. God, you are my buckler." I could not move past it. For some reason, God wanted me to focus on that part. Honestly I did not know what a buckler was, so I did some research. A buckler is a small portable shield for protection. It is worn around the arm and is useful in deflecting the blows of an enemy. It is not cumbersome like shields carried on the battlefield, but it is lightweight and can be worn daily. God wanted me to know that He is my shield. He will protect me when the Enemy hurls insults at me. When he attempts to demean and degrade me, God will cover me.

No one was more humiliated than Jesus, who endured suffering and the shame of the cross. They found witnesses who falsely accused Him (Matthew 26:60–61). When asked by the high priest if the accusations were true, Jesus did not respond until further urged to do so. Appalled at His response, the high priest commanded they strip Him of His clothes. They spit on Him and hit Him repeatedly. The soldiers mocked and taunted Him as they crowned Him with thorns. They plucked His beard. He was despised and rejected (Isaiah 53:3). They beat Him until He was unrecognizable. To add further insult, they nailed Him to the cross—the emblem of shame. He hung there for all to see as they passed by and reviled Him. So who understands humiliation more than Jesus? He knows what it is like to be humiliated before a crowd, to be disgraced, and to be asked an embarrassing question.

The Enemy accomplished his intent to embarrass me, but he failed at crushing my spirit. He wanted me to walk in fear, but God has not given us a spirit of fear (2 Timothy 1:7). He gave me knowledge, and through that knowledge, He gave me power—power to stand before a class full of ruthless and sometimes heartless middle schoolers. Those scenarios I used to replay in my mind that crippled me with fear were no longer on repeat. Now I embraced a new scenario. I would stand at attention before the class with my invisible buckler ready to defend me at all costs. I would not run. I would not retreat. I would stand my ground and let my buckler protect me.

What the Enemy means for evil, God will turn around for good. We do not have to walk in fear and allow it to control our lives. Exchange fear for confidence—not confidence in ourselves but in God. I had no self-confidence. My self-esteem had suffered many debilitating punches. I told myself, *You're bald; you're ugly; you're not good enough.* I learned to bob and weave to avoid some of the jabs intended to knock me out, but God's Word says, "Though an army besiege me, my heart will not fear; though war break out against me, even then I will be confident" (Psalm 27:3 NIV).

Whatever your situation is, refuse Satan's lies. So here you go, fear. We serve you notice today. We refuse to accept the lies you're selling. We are who God says we are, and we put our confidence in Him.

> The Lord is my rock, and my fortress, and my deliverer; my God, my strength, in whom I will trust; my buckler, and the horn of my salvation, and my high tower. (Psalm 18:2 KJV)

> But the Lord is my defence; and my God is the rock of my refuge. (Psalm 94:22 KJV)

ABOUT THE SONG

I remember when my kids, Kimmel and Kimmaya, were younger. Being eight years apart in age, they didn't share in many activities. One day Kimmaya was outside playing with friends. An older boy was riding his bike down the street and called her a bad name. She ran in the house to her brother and said, "Bubba," which she so lovingly called him, "this big boy called me out on my name." Kimmel jumped to his feet. "Who is he? Show me who he is." He went outside to defend his little sister, but the boy could not be found.

God comes to our rescue, just like my son did for my daughter. God is our defender and our protector who keeps us safe from all harm. We have to be like my daughter and have faith that He will protect and cover us from the Enemy.

Defender

Verse 1
When the terror strike at night
When the arrows pierce the day
When darkness surrounds me
When destruction comes my way.

Chorus
You are my defender
You are my protector
You are my God
In you I trust
Keep me safe from the Enemy
Protect me from dangers and disease
Shelter me underneath your wings
You are my defender.

Verse 2

You'll be with me in trouble
You will answer when I call
You'll rescue and save me
You will catch me when I fall.

Bridge

I am not afraid
I am not afraid
I'm safe in your arms.

CHAPTER 7

Identity Crisis

I FINALLY SETTLED INTO MY REALITY that I would have to wear wigs for the rest of my life. I felt a prisoner to my shame. My wig was less an accessory and more of a vital part of my life. I could not go anywhere or do anything without my wig. If the doorbell rang for a package or pizza delivery, I'd scramble to get my wig, which usually meant making a mad dash to my bedroom, awkwardly throwing the wig on my head, and quickly straightening the disheveled mess. I'm sure I answered the door with my wig on backward more than a time or two. Although I had overcome the fear of wearing or losing my wig, now I faced the bondage of wearing it. Not just the outward bondage but the inward shackles that attacked my self-identity, self-esteem, and self-worth.

Crisis is "the point in a play or story at which hostile elements are most tensely opposed to each other" (www.dictionary.com). I was in crisis mode, with two opposing forces. The *me* I was—that person who was a prisoner to wearing wigs—and the *me* I wanted to be— that person who wanted my own hair. The irony of my childhood days resurfaced when I had wanted long, shaky hair cascading down my back. Now I just wanted hair. It didn't matter the length or the texture, I just wanted hair. The daily struggle felt endless. The battle to salvage what little self-worth I had started as soon as I faced a mirror. Everything was okay until that point.

I woke up for my morning prayer, worship, and Bible reading to arm myself against what I would encounter from the Enemy. I failed to realize the Enemy was not my attacker. The attack originated from within me. It was self-sabotage, a self-imposed bondage of hatred. I loathed my appearance. *How could anyone love me looking like this?* By this time I was totally bald on top of my head. I think tension caused by the braiding and me ripping out the glued-in weave tracks contributed to this condition. For whatever reason, I still had hair— and can still grow hair—along the back of my head, but on top there was nothing. Nada. Zilch. Not even a hint of hair. No open hair follicles for which hair could sprout. My head, smooth as a baby's bottom, tormented me as I looked in the mirror to see the real me. I felt ashamed and humiliated and overwhelmed. It made me sick to my stomach. Instead of looking at my disgusting, bald head in the mirror, I would quickly put on my wig cap.

Each day I plummeted further and further into my self-imposed bondage and even got to a point where I would not allow my husband or children to see the shame of my bald head. I lived in my wig twenty-four hours, seven days a week. It took up residence on my head. I didn't move or breathe without it. I felt like Linus in the *Peanuts* comic strip, who carried a security blanket everywhere he went. He could not survive without it. If he didn't have his blanket, he would have a panic attack. My wig was my security blanket. I couldn't imagine being without it. Linus's blanket transformed and was used for purposes other than for comfort. He used it for a stylish neck scarf, big bow tie, and even an insect swapper. Linus was not embarrassed by the need for his blanket. I needed my wig, but unlike Linus, I was highly embarrassed and ashamed.

As a child I recall playing make-believe, fantasizing that I had long hair by placing a towel or yarn on my head. Now I just fantasized about having any hair at all. Maybe my wig could somehow magically fuse to my scalp and would begin to take root and grow as my own hair. I know it sounds silly and childish, but I was desperate. I'd try anything at this point. Someone suggested that I massage my scalp daily to stimulate hair growth. I tried that. I tried Rogaine. It was recommended by dermatologists and clinically proven to boost hair growth by targeting hair follicles to reactivate hair growth. I needed reactivation, so without consulting an expert, I spent several hundred dollars hoping that it would work for me. It didn't. My hair follicles needed more than reactivation. They needed resurrection. And I was still willing to try almost anything. I saw a commercial for Bosley, the hair transplant specialist, and rushed to schedule a consultation. At this point, I didn't care if a professional saw my bald head if by some chance they could help. Maybe this was the answer. Wrong. My hope vanished quickly. After explaining the procedure to me, the consultant said, "Unfortunately, you are not a candidate for this hair transplant procedure."

I was confused. Who, if not me, would be a better candidate? I had no hair. That was the problem. I didn't have enough hair at the back of my head to harvest and transplant to cover my entire head. I left dejected and brokenhearted at the news that there was no help for me. Besides a miracle from God, I would have to live the rest of my life bald.

I cried many tears after that consultation. I had gone to that appointment optimistic, hopeful that I had found the solution to my baldness, but had returned hopeless, sinking further into my self-imposed bondage and into my own personal black hole. Like gravity, depression pulled me further and further into a place of no escape, a place of darkness. Besides feeling lost and alone, I felt abandoned, as if God had let me down. I would never allow myself to speak this aloud, but inwardly I had a lot to say and accused God for my situation. *How could He allow this to happen to me?*

Many years in church taught me not to question God, but I did take a play from Job's playbook (Job 30:18–25). Like Job, I laid out all the things I'd done for God. I had served Him most of my adult life. I tried to live by His standards. I traveled for the ministry. I sang His praises until I had no voice. I gave my money above and beyond tithes and offerings. I labored in the house of God to minister and care for His people. I studied His Word and prayed often. I practically took up residence at my church, because I was there just as much as I was at my own home. Was I blaming God? I knew better than to do that. It wasn't God's fault (John 10:10), but I was definitely complaining. I just wanted Him to fix it. I wanted Him to give me a miracle so my hair would grow back, because that was what it would take.

The years continued to go by, and still no miracle. I prayed many prayers for healing and got in countless prayer lines, but I received nothing. No amount of oil or laying on of hands changed anything. I was still bald. *Was I being punished for something I did or didn't do?* I began to search the recesses of my memory for some transgression of the Scripture or violation of the Spirit, scrutinizing each page of my life in an attempt to ascertain some reason why I was bald. Well, there was that time when I gave the cashier a piece of my mind in a not-so-kind tone. Or maybe it was the time I didn't give a soft answer to my husband, and the disagreement escalated into a one-sided screaming match with me doing all of the screaming. Could it have been the time when that man cut me off in traffic, and I made a not-so-nice gesture toward him? Back and forth over and over, I replayed pictures in my mind, pushing the rewind button to make sure I didn't miss anything. It was overwhelming and exhausting. My mind was on overload. *This had to be the reason I was bald, right?*

In Bible times, it was a common fallacy to think that sickness or infirmities were a result of sin. In John 9, Jesus saw a blind man. His disciples asked Him who had sinned, the man or his parents. Jesus cleared up the fallacy and told His disciples that neither had sinned, but the man was blind so that the glory of God could be revealed. I could stop tormenting myself thinking I had done something wrong. "He does not treat us as our sins deserve or repay us according to our iniquities" (Psalm 103:10 NIV). God is gracious and compassionate. Understanding His character put my mind at ease, and although I had done some things that were questionable and displeasing to God, these things did not result in my baldness.

Not only did I search inwardly for the answer, but I also searched the Scriptures for the reason for my baldness. Maybe I had become too proud, like the women of Zion in Isaiah 3. They strutted around with their heads in the air, swinging their hips back and forth to draw attention to their outward beauty. They adorned themselves with jewelry and anklets to draw attention to themselves. For this reason, the Lord brought sores on their scalps, resulting in baldness (3:16–24). This couldn't be the reason for my baldness. When I did have hair, I was never conceited. As a curvy woman, I would rather hide in the shadows than draw attention to myself. I never dressed immodestly, and I was very unassuming. I still grappled for the answer to my baldness and came up short.

In 1 Corinthians 11, Paul says a woman's hair is her glory. Since I had no hair, did that mean I had no glory? I wrestled with this Scripture for a long time, feeling as though I were less of a person— less of a woman. Hair is such a big part of our identity as women. It symbolizes our femininity. It is one attribute that makes us feel attractive and pretty. It is the crown we never take off. Often it is what people first notice about us. It is our most identifiable feature. Now all they noticed about me was my wig. I felt insecure and self-conscious, always thinking people were staring at me. I never realized the boost of confidence gained from having hair until mine was gone. No hair resulted in no confidence, lost femininity, and lost identity.

It didn't help that the church I was a member of supported the idea that women should have long hair. A very close friend of mine had beautiful, long, wavy hair. Of course the longer it grew, the less manageable it was, so she decided that she would cut it all off. She did not just cut off an inch or two to the shoulders, she got a school-boy cut. It was a drastic change. "Oh, my goodness," I exclaimed, "I can't believe you cut your hair." I was happy for her, yet dismayed. It seemed like everyone who was blessed to have beautiful hair would just chop it off without hesitation. If only I had that choice. Then she said four words that made me cringe. "It will grow back," she said without a doubt. She often joked how her hair grew like grass.

A dichotomy of emotions swirled in my mind. If only that were a true statement for me. But at the same time, I loved her new look.

"You like it?" she asked, beaming with excitement.

Of course, I loved it, and so did everyone else.

She sported that hairstyle for many months and even took it a little shorter, until one day in front of the entire church assembly, she was told to stop cutting her hair. She was told that cutting the hair too short could open the door for the wrong spirit to overtake her mind. In reality, this person preferred women with long hair. The mild rebuke of her actions ended with the statement that men want women with long hair. It is shameful when someone allows their personal opinions to manipulate and discourage the desires of others. It is no one else's business how a woman wears her hair, and it certainly should not be mentioned from the pulpit. My translation of the mild rebuke was that no man wants a bald woman, which meant no man wanted me because I was bald. I sat there embarrassed for my friend while inwardly trembling, hiding under my wig, afraid that this displeasure would somehow find me. All the while the words were on repeat in my ears: *no man wants a bald woman; no man wants a bald woman.* I wondered if this was the opinion of my husband. *Had I married a man who was shallow and superficial and who thought this way?*

Being bald had a tremendous impact on my relationship with my husband. We had taken vows to love and honor one another in sickness and in health—but not in baldness. There were times when I felt he would be justified if he just walked away and times when I expected him to look at me in disgust and disapproval, but he never did. My husband upheld his end of the bargain. He didn't marry me for my hair. He never looked at me differently, nor was he disgusted by my appearance. I was the one with the problem. I took all my feelings and anxiety and placed them on him, as if he were the one who had the issue. He didn't care, but in my mind he hadn't agreed to this. Baldness was not a part of the package deal. I felt sorry for him because he was stuck with me. I'm sure his friends laughed when they saw us together, but together we were. He never left my side, even though I separated myself from him emotionally. At this point, we had been married for fourteen years, yet I thought he was repulsed by me.

I put up emotional barriers to prevent myself from being hurt if he decided he couldn't handle me being bald. I would not allow myself to get close to him. We were still intimate, but there was an emotional detachment on my part. *How could he want me with no hair?* He could no longer run his fingers through my hair. If he did, he would pull off my wig. That would have been a turn-off for sure. There was also a physical barrier. I remember the days when we shared the bathroom mirror while getting dressed. Him brushing his teeth and combing his hair and me putting on makeup. We would chat about our plans for the day or what we would have for dinner. Those days were over now.

I came to a point in my journey where I would no longer allow him to see me without something covering my head. I kept the bathroom door locked so he could not enter. I made a stranger out of the person with whom I intimately shared most of my adult life.

We never discussed my baldness, so I never knew what he thought about it, and I didn't want to know. In my heart, I knew he was with me till death do us part, although I secretly wanted him to free himself from my shame. I thought he deserved so much better than what I'd become—a bitter, depressed bald woman. I tried to make life uncomfortable and unbearable for him by pushing him away. But he endured. I'd go weeks without speaking to him, trying to break him, but he was unbreakable. He never once lashed out at me or called me names. He definitely was not one of those shallow, superficial men I encountered in church who cared about the outward appearance more than the soul. My husband was the real deal.

There is another who is not concerned about our outward appearance. He does not see the color of our skin, the shape of our bodies, or the length of our hair. He sees the real you. He has a bird's-eye view into your heart, and it's not clouded by opinions or preferences. First Samuel 16:7 (NIV) says, "The Lord does not look at the things people look at. People look at the outward appearance, but the Lord looks at the heart." That's a beautiful thing to know. God looks beyond our faults, failures, flaws, insecurities, depression, and anxiety. He transcends those things and goes directly to the heart of the matter to address our needs. Not only does He see what we need, but He is also able to satisfy that need. God reminded me through my husband's *stick-to-itiveness* that He would never leave me or abandon me, and God is not a promise breaker. God will not walk out when our beauty fades, when the wrinkles appear, or when the hairline recedes. That's not what He sees. God loves us for who we are and not for how we look. Underneath all our disguises, He sees a fragile heart. Beneath all our facades, He sees our brokenness and pain. Rest assured, He will not turn His back on us. He is faithful even when we are faithless (2 Timothy 2:13). No matter what you go through, trust that He will be there through it all.

> For God has said, "I will never leave you; I will never abandon you." Let us be bold, then, and say, "The Lord is my helper, I will not be afraid. What can anyone do to me?" (Hebrews 13:5b–6 GNT)

ABOUT THE SONG

All of us have a story to tell. A story of highs and lows and ups and downs, but through it all we can still stand like the palm tree in a storm. It bends and bows but rarely is uprooted. It may have some bumps and bruises from the storm, but it's still standing. This is a song of perseverance, overcoming the hardships of life, and learning to trust God at all costs. He won't let us down.

Through It All

Verse 1
It's easy to say thanks
For the blessings we receive
But when the trials come
That knocks us to our knees
We look up to heaven
And wonder what went wrong
God says in our weakness
He will make us strong.

Chorus
Through it all I will trust in Jesus
Through it all He promise He'd be there
Every valley every mountain
I know it's in His plan
Thank You, Jesus (3x)
You are right there through it all.

Verse 2
When life seems problem free
And prosperity increase
But when the tables turn
And there's no food to eat
Praise Him for this season
From ashes, He brings joy

Weeping may last one night
When morning comes rejoice.

Bridge
Through it all, through it all,
through it all I will trust in His Word.

CHAPTER 8

Let It Rain

APRIL 2018 WAS A TURNING POINT in my journey. My journey started almost thirty years ago, for which the last ten left me in confinement, sentenced to wearing hot, itchy, sweaty wigs for the rest of my life. I felt like a prisoner, and the wig was my shackle.

Even inmates on death row get an hour outside to breathe the fresh air and get some sunlight, but not me. Except for showers, I was in bondage to that wig twenty-four hours a day. My wig was my identity and who I had become—an insecure woman content to live in the comfort of a cocoon that protected me from my truth. But something was shifting. God was overturning my sentence. Although He repealed my verdict, I struggled with accepting my freedom for another year.

Wig or not, I've always wanted to live my life in such a way that God could get the glory. This was a daily petition that began even before I was confined to wearing wigs. I ask God to use me to minister in word or song and that people see Him and not me—that He would become more important and I become less important (John 3:30). One morning in prayer, after I put this petition before Him, the thought came to me to let go of my wig—to take it off and just be myself. I must admit I didn't know the origin of this thought. I didn't know if it was a result of my desire to be free of the bondage I was in or if it was really the voice of the Lord. I did not dismiss the idea or share it with anyone right away. I just thought deeply about the notion of taking off my wig.

The very thought of doing it terrified me, and I had a hundred thoughts bombarding my mind on a daily basis. *What would I look like? How would I feel? What would people say? Surely they would laugh at me and mock me for being bald-headed. Children would point in curiosity. Women would look with pity. Men would stare with contempt. Would my children be embarrassed to be seen with me? Would my husband be ashamed to hold my hand in public?*

Oddly enough, the more I pondered it, the more courage I gained. I finally mustered up enough of it to share the idea with my husband and children. One evening while sitting in our family room, I casually posed the question to them. My husband was watching TV, and my children and I were playing a game. I asked, "How would you feel if I decided to take off my wig, shave what hair I have left, and just walk around bald with no scarf or hat—just bald?"

The more my family voiced their SUPPORT, the MORE CONFIDENCE I gained. I was going to do it. I would TAKE MY WIG OFF and just be my bald, BEAUTIFUL SELF.

At first they were silent, each one hesitantly awaiting the other's response. My husband turned toward me with a look of confusion. He asked, "What do you mean?"

I responded, "I mean would you be embarrassed by my appearance?" Then, unlike the silence before, a blitz of affirmations flooded the room:

"Absolutely not."

"No way we're embarrassed by you."

"Do what makes you feel good."

Not one of my children gave me a discouraging word. They all encouraged me to do it. "We got your back, Mom. We love you no matter what," my kids said.

My husband chimed in. "You'll still be beautiful to me."

That was it. That was just what I needed to hear. My family would be supportive. The more my family voiced their support, the more confidence I gained. I was going to do it. I would take my wig off and just be my bald, beautiful self.

I had worn a wig for about fifteen years. I began to think about how life would be without one. I would not have to worry about a gust of wind whisking it off my head or about my students' curiosity. I could go to the water park, and instead of being confined to the lazy river, I could live dangerously and slide down the waterslide. *Oh what joy and liberty I would have without that wig!* Imagining life without it was exciting and frightening. But I couldn't let that deter me. I felt like the little engine that could. *I think I can. I think I can do this.* But what would be the alternative? I didn't have any hair on the top of my head. I surely wasn't going to go around looking like Bozo the Clown.

I would have to shave my head and go bald. Bald? That was the alternative? That was unimaginable. I'd be crazy to do something like that. To set myself up for ridicule, to be the brunt of jokes? Absolutely not. There was a game of tug-of-war playing in my mind, going back and forth between two choices, but fear crept in, and I rejected the thought of taking off my wig. I dismissed what I thought was the voice of God as my own. It must have been my desire, my fantasy speaking through me. Surely God wouldn't want me to be a laughingstock for people to mock and ridicule.

I had hope of freedom from that wig for a brief period, until fear robbed me of it, just like Peter walking on water (Matthew 14:22–33). First Peter had the audacity to ask Jesus if he could come to him on the water, and then he had the faith to act upon his request. He stepped out of the boat into an uncertain situation not knowing what to expect. Imagine what was going through his mind as he began to put one foot in front of the other. At first, he was probably amazed that he too could defy the laws of physics and walk on water. With each step toward Jesus, Peter gained more and more confidence—until he doubted. What caused Peter to doubt? The text states that Peter saw the wind, and it caused him to fear. But he was already aware of the wind, for when Jesus told the disciples to get in the boat and go to the other side, the winds were already raging, causing the waves to crash against the boat (Matthew 14:24). Could it have been that Peter allowed what he thought others would say to cause him to doubt? Maybe he thought the other disciples would think he was crazy, or maybe he thought the other disciples would accuse him of being arrogant. Whatever the reason, Peter doubted and succumbed to fear.

Like Peter, I had allowed fear to get the best of me. I sank back into my comfort zone, my Linus blanket. Wearing my wig was a familiar space and comfortable for me, even though I hated wearing it. I knew what to expect when I wore it. I knew people would not ridicule me for my looks. I didn't have to worry about disparaging comments. Although I walked in fear of losing my wig, the fear of being exposed was far greater.

Life continued for another year with me bound to some type of wig, whether short, long, brown, black, wavy, or straight. It became my identity. When I felt playful, I would wear my whimsical, wavy wig I affectionately called *Wendy*. When I felt sexy, I would wear *Sasha*, my silky, straight wig. I could be a different person every day. My husband would comment that he had a new lady whenever I'd wear a different wig. I looked different on the outside, but I was bound on the inside. No matter how much I pretended to be *Wendy* or *Sasha*, I was still Carol, and I was bald. My identity was obscured by my many years confined to a wig, and I needed to find myself, my true identity. *Who was I, where did I belong, and what did God want for me?* I was clueless to His plan and His purpose for my life. I never imagined that finding my true identity would lead me to reveal that I was bald.

Exactly one year after I had the thought to take off my wig, I started to again have the same thoughts, only they were stronger this time. Day after day, my mind flooded with thoughts of living without my wig, and like a movie, scenes continuously played in my mind. I consulted my family again. They were still very supportive, but I think a little aggravated by the same question I had posed to them the year before. Their consensus was, "If you're going to do it, do it. We got your back."

It was a Saturday morning, and I was home alone. As was my custom, I got up early for prayer and Bible reading. As always, I laid my usual petition before God, "Lord, I want you to get the glory in my life." But this time was different. Sometimes we look for God to pass by one way, but He's not in the wind, the fire, or an earthquake (1 Kings 19:11–12). This time it wasn't a thought, but a still small voice. It was undeniable. God audibly said, "How can I get the glory if they never know your struggle?" The voice was so crystal clear that I couldn't explain it away as a thought this time. It was the voice of the Lord. Tears began to stream down my face. Now it was obvious to me that God wanted me to take my wig off and walk in the light of His glory.

For an entire year, I had walked in disobedience to His will and continued my self-imposed bondage and hopelessness when God wanted to deliver me. An unexplainable peace and calmness now consumed me. I knew exactly what I had to do. I had to let go of my security blanket. I had to stop pretending to be *Wendy* and *Sasha* and allow God to do His perfect work through me, so that He could receive the glory. It was time for me to be the real me, find my true identity, and walk in His purpose. I could have resisted, but instead I humbled myself and said yes to His will.

I stood to my feet, walked into my bathroom, and stared at my reflection in the mirror. Of course, the Enemy tried to convince me not to do it. He wanted me to continue with my self-imposed bondage that would keep me from fulfilling God's purpose for my life. But this time I was determined, convinced I had heard the voice of the Lord. There was no going back.

I yanked off my wig and proceeded with my mission. I grabbed a pair of scissors and began to cut the hair on the back of my head. Then I grabbed my husband's clippers and shaved what was left.

I rubbed my hand across the back of my head. It was all gone. What used to be a coarse, hairy texture was now as smooth as a baby's bottom, just like the top of my head. There, it was done.

I gasped in panic questioning what I had done, but the panic soon turned to joy. I smiled at myself. This was the first time in years that I looked in the mirror with nothing covering my bald head. I smiled. I felt liberated, like a boulder had been lifted off.

"Girl," I giggled to myself, "you look good." I kept staring at my transformation, still processing the difference. I decided to put on makeup to get the full effect. I said, "Girl, you don't look bad at all." I had worn wigs for so long, I had forgotten how blessed I was with great facial features. The wig had hidden my large almond-shaped eyes and high cheekbones. I felt good about myself.

Pleased with the outcome, I went to my music room and sat at my piano. I began to softly play and sing. After a few minutes, it began to rain. The Lord asked me, "What does the rain represent?" I thought about it a moment as I gazed out of the window watching the rain droplets form on the window. He repeated the question. I began to shed tears of joy. It was as if I were peering directly into God's heart, seeing myself for the first time.

He reminded me that rain washes away debris and trash— discarded things. Rain represents renewal and revival of what was once dead. It represents cleansing. It's a washing away of the old so the new can spring forth. When I was a child, my friends and I would play in the rain. I remember watching the rain carry broken twigs and trash alongside the curb until they disappeared down the sewage drain. That was what God did for me. He washed away the ugliness of baldness and exchanged it for beauty. He turned my shame into glory and my humiliation into honor (Proverbs 15:33).

We all experience ugliness in our lives that grips us with fear and paralyzes us with shame. God wants to send the rain to wash it away. We allow the Enemy to manipulate and convince us that we are not pretty, that things won't change, that we are worthless, and the list goes on. If you're like me, you believed his lies for too long, accepting them as our truth. But the lies are not true, my friends. Satan lied from the beginning, deceiving Eve into thinking she could be what God never intended for her to be. He continues to lie and deceive us into thinking we can't be what God intends for us to be. The truth is we are fearfully and wonderfully made by God no matter what we look like (Psalm 139:14). Notice the Scripture does not state we are fearfully and wonderfully and beautifully made. God does not put emphasis on outward beauty as man does.

The Enemy set a benchmark for beauty, and we struggle daily to reach it, like hamsters chasing a ball around the wheel—constantly chasing the idea of beauty but always falling short, because beauty is not the benchmark. The Enemy has us chasing the abstract when all we have to do is accept the fact that we are fearfully and wonderfully made by a loving Creator. He doesn't make ugliness. He doesn't make junk to be discarded with the trash. The Hebrew word for fearfully is *yare* (Strongs #3372), which, according to Vine's Dictionary, means "to be honored" or "awesome." We are awesomely made, so we can stop trying to measure up to an unattainable idea and instead embrace God's truth.

> I will praise thee; for I am fearfully and wonderfully made: marvelous are thy works; and that my soul knoweth right well. (Psalms 139:14 KJV)

ABOUT THE SONG

God gave me this song right after my bold reveal. Sometimes I write songs from pictures I see in my mind. "Wonderfully Made" was one of those songs. It was as if I were watching a movie of my life over and over again—the pain of being excluded and the disgust I felt when I looked in the mirror, to finally the victory of discovering my true identity. No matter where we come from, how we look, or what our background is, God's works are altogether wonderfully made, and He doesn't make mistakes.

Wonderfully Made

Verse 1
There in the mirror
Staring at me
Someone I don't
Want to be
Trying to pretend
Wanting to fit in
Scared they will see
The real me.

Pre-Chorus
You formed me with Your hand
Before time began
You had me in Your plan.

Chorus
I'm fearfully and wonderfully made
A picture of Your beauty and grace
A beautiful masterpiece
Molded in Your love
I'm fearfully and wonderfully made.

Verse 2
All the wasted time
Hiding my shame
Invisible but
You knew me
Alone and afraid
Imperfect and flawed
You still loved me
Just the same.

Pre-Chorus
You formed me with Your hand
Before time began
You had me in Your plan.

Bridge
Your works are altogether wonderfully made
No matter what others say, God does not make mistakes.

CHAPTER 9

The Aftermath

FREEDOM. YOU DON'T REALIZE HOW BOUND you are until you are set free. That's exactly what I experienced—freedom that ignited a state of euphoria and intense happiness and self-confidence gained from walking in the light of God's glory. I am free, liberated from the confinement of wigs and self-loathing. Free to be myself. Free to love myself. Free to be what God wants me to be. There are no more chains gripping me in fear. I am no longer shackled by shame but am now led by freedom.

I decided to celebrate my newfound freedom with a professional photo shoot. I coined the phrase "I have alopecia, but it doesn't have me," and I captured it on a T-shirt for my photo session, announcing to the world that I was no longer a prisoner to my shame. The photo shoot was on location at the riverfront pier, which required me to be outside. It was the first time I'd leave my house as a bald woman. I didn't know what to expect, so I was a little apprehensive and afraid. *What would people say? Would they laugh at me or look at me with contempt?* As I was getting dressed, I thought about calling the whole thing off, but that was not an option. I told God I'd do this, so there was no turning back.

I proceeded to the location for my photo shoot feeling a bit nervous. It was an early morning appointment, so I didn't think there would be too many people who would see me. I couldn't have been more wrong. It seemed like hundreds of people were out that morning, pouring out of cars to walk on the pier, riding bikes, skating on sidewalks. People were everywhere. I wondered, *Why aren't they asleep or getting ready for work?* I sat in my car for a few minutes before stepping out to meet the photographer. I felt naked and vulnerable without my wig, but I had to do it. I mustered up enough courage to open the car door. I swung my legs outside the car, placed my feet on the pavement, and catapulted my body outside the car, all in one motion, to defeat the thoughts in my mind of turning around and going back home. There, I did it.

I stood outside of my car and let the world see my perfectly shaped, brown, bald head. It was exhilarating. I felt like a prisoner just released from years of solitary confinement. It was as if I were breathing fresh air for the first time and hearing the melodic sounds of singing birds. As the sunrise unveiled a clear, blue sky, it brought new revelation. Psalm 19:1 says, "The heavens declare the glory of God, and the sky displays what his hands have made." Just as God's glory is manifested through a brilliant sky, it is also manifested in me—with or without hair.

The photographer approached me. She said, "You must be Carol." What gave it away? It was probably the fact that I was the only bald woman there.

I responded, "Yes" and extended my hand to greet her.

She said, "You look amazing. You're going to look great in these photos." *She probably tells all her clients the same thing. Was she just trying to make me feel good about myself?* Well it worked. Her words gave me the confidence I needed to pose for those pictures. With each click of the lens, I gained more and more confidence.

May 2, 2019, was the big reveal day. I woke up thrilled but nervous about posting my pictures to social media platforms. I carefully selected the best poses from dozens of photos taken; now I was ready to hit the send button.

I hesitated a bit because once the photos were on social media, they would be visible to hundreds of my friends and followers. Before I realized it, my finger pressed that send button, and the photos were posted. Immediately I started receiving notifications. People expressed their approval with the like and love emojis. The comments were invigorating. There was not one negative comment.

"You look beautiful."

"You are stunning."

"I never knew you had alopecia."

My favorite was, "Where have you been hiding those cheekbones?"

All the comments were so encouraging. It was an emotional day. I cried tears of joy practically all day long. Every time I opened a social media app, a new stream of tears. The reality of the results surpassed my expectations. I did not expect the outpouring of love and support I received.

My big reveal opened a new community for me, filled with new and exciting opportunities to bond with others who understood what it was like to be bald. I began to receive friend requests from other bald women who became my cheerleaders. Sometimes when you're walking in despair, you fail to realize you are not alone and that there are others who have walked the journey before you.

A social media reveal is far different from an in-person reveal. I could delete social media comments and block commenters, but what could I expect from face-to-face encounters? I went to the grocery store the day following my big reveal. I proudly and confidently wore my T-shirt with my coined phrase. My husband accompanied me to the store, and his strong presence offered me a sense of security. I was confident no one would say a disparaging word to me with my husband present. I felt like a little kid who has been bullied by his peers, but when his big brother is with him, he knows the bully won't confront him, so he walks with his chest out and his head held high. That's exactly how I felt. It was as if I dared anyone to say anything. I walked through the grocery store up and down each aisle. I purposely looked people in the face while greeting them. I made direct eye contact with shoppers passing by. *Were they avoiding me? Were they just grossed out by a bald woman?* It was if I were screaming inside, "Look at me, look at me." Finally a lady engaged me in conversation. I thought, *She's looking at me. Brace yourself; here comes the negative comment.*

Instead she complimented my shirt. *Is that all? Is she oblivious to my bald head?* Clearly she saw me. At that moment, I discovered something about people—they really don't care. They have their own flaws and insecurities. Mine just happens to be visible. People are consumed with their own lives, and they don't have the mental capacity or the time to take on anyone else's problems.

The next day would be the real challenge for me. I figured no one said anything negative to me the day before because my husband accompanied me to the store. I wanted to do a little shopping, but my husband was unable to go with me this time. I had to venture out on my own. I agonized over him not going with me. I needed him to protect me, to cover me. Filled with anxiety, I continued preparing to leave the house. I thought that I'd just put on a cute headwrap, but conflict raged inside me. I was certain God wanted me to do this without any covering for my head. He wants to set us free from bondage—not just bondage from sin but the residual effects of sin that plague us inwardly. I was trying to hold on to what God wanted to strip from me. He wanted me to trust His plan, which is not always easy.

I left the house on my way to the unknown, unsure of what I would encounter. I was nervous and afraid. Even pulling up next to another car at the stoplight was scary. I sat, staring straight ahead. I couldn't bring myself to glance at the car next to me. It seemed the light took forever to turn green. Thank God it finally changed, and I didn't hesitate to press my foot on the gas pedal only to have to stop at the next light. It seemed I stopped at every single traffic light that day.

I finally made it to my first shopping location. Unlike my grocery store experience, I was less confident and didn't feel safe at all. I felt like there was a target on my back, just beckoning for ridicule and insults to take aim. The vulnerability was overwhelming.

I sat in my car in fear, trembling at the idea of going in the store alone, unprotected by my companion. It took a few minutes for me to muster the strength to open the car door and step out into the unknown. Each step I took brought me closer to the store entrance, but inwardly I took a half step back toward my car. With each step it became harder to lift my feet, like they were glued to the pavement. I was walking the long green mile. *Will I ever make it to the entrance of the store?* Then I heard the Spirit whisper, "I am with you," and immediately billows of peace swept over me. The whispers echoed over and over, "I am with you." I was reminded of the Scripture in Deuteronomy 31:6 (NIV), "Be strong and courageous. Do not be afraid or terrified because of them, for the Lord your God goes with you; he will never leave you nor forsake you." Yes, if God told me to do it, He would be with me. My job was to be strong and courageous, so my feet felt lighter and my steps more intentional. My confidence grew with each stride. Before long, I was walking through the entrance of the store.

I began to browse through the store and found a few items. If anyone did say anything negative, I was oblivious to it. I knew God was with me. I proceeded to the checkout counter. While standing in line, there was a lady with two small girls directly in front of me. They were probably about six or seven years old. One was blond and the other brunette. Their clothes were a little soiled from playing outside, and they were barefoot. I was somewhat disgusted that they were barefoot. *Who would bring their kids to the store with no shoes?* The lady moved to the counter to pay for her merchandise, but the girls lingered in front of me. One of them looked at me and whispered in the other girl's ear. Then they both turned around and stared at me. I thought, *Okay here we go.* It was clear to me that they were talking about me and maybe a little curious about my appearance, so I braced myself for what they would say. You know kids say the darndest things, so I waited, prepared to take the blow.

One of the girls said, "I like your earrings." *Really? That's why they were looking intensely and whispering?* To my surprise, they said nothing about my bald head. I asked them their names. They introduced themselves and told me how old they were. They began to engage in conversation about school and the number of pets they had. One of them said, "I have a pet rabbit."

I said, "Wow, I had a pet rabbit as a kid, and a chicken too." They were intrigued about my pet chicken but not one word about my bald head. This conversation continued until their mom completed her purchase. As they were leaving they turned to tell me goodbye, and still no mention of why I didn't have any hair.

What was I supposed to learn from this experience? I believe God was teaching me to view others from the perspective of a child. Those girls saw that I was different but didn't judge me based on my appearance. They didn't allow our differences to keep them from talking to me. I realized I was not giving people the opportunity to see me—the real me. I had written them off, convinced they would laugh at me or say mean things about me. I was afraid they would judge me because I looked different, when I had actually judged them for not wearing shoes. I learned a valuable lesson that day: to embrace my own flaws and imperfections and accept the differences of others.

With each step taken that day, I gained more confidence; however, I knew my next stop would be the real challenge. I went to the mall, where I visited more stores and encountered more people, which increased the likelihood of being ridiculed. But I was less nervous and afraid than I had started my day. I was not intimidated when I stopped at traffic lights. This time when I parked my car, there was no lingering in fear before exiting the vehicle. Confidence engulfed me. Boldness enveloped me. When shopping the day before with my husband, I felt safe, protected, covered, strong, and fearless. I felt the same today, comforted knowing that though I was by myself, I was not alone.

I boldly walked into the mall entrance with my beautiful, bald head. Every step I took exuded confidence. My smile was infectious and so contagious that people could not help but smile back.

I wondered what was going through their mind. *Why is she bald? Wow, she's bold. There's no way I could do that.* Whatever they were thinking, they kept it to themselves, smiled back at me, and continued walking.

I went to one of the stores and started to shop. It wasn't long before I found something I liked. As I was standing in line to purchase the item, I noticed an older woman walking toward me, staring intently. She was an attractive older woman, well dressed in a tailored suit with pearl accessories and long, silvery hair pulled back from her face. As she got closer, her stares made me feel a little uncomfortable.

I looked away to avoid her gaze, but when I turned backed, she was still staring at me. At this point, I was more than uncomfortable. I was deeply disturbed. There were so many people around. I didn't want her to say anything to embarrass me. I wanted to drop what was in my hand and run before she approached me, but I stood my ground.

She said, "Excuse me."

Hesitantly I responded, "Yes ma'am."

She said, "I saw you as I walked from the other side of the store and couldn't take my eyes off you. You are absolutely gorgeous."

I was flabbergasted. I didn't expect this at all. I felt beautiful. "Thank you so much," and right then in the middle of the store, I began to share my testimony with her.

She stood in amazement listening as if she were hanging on to every word I said, her eyes surveying me like a painter studies a canvas. I knew I was not standing there alone. God was with me, strengthening and empowering me to walk in the light of His glory. I realized I had exchanged the security of my wig for the security of my husband, but God wanted to be my security and my protector.

If we dwell in Him, He promises to be our shield from the negativity of the world and from every negative comment the Enemy speaks directly to us to crush our self-image. We have all been overwhelmed by our insecurities, imperfections, and flaws. Satan preys on this to cause self-doubt and fear. Yes, I said *preys*. He seizes our self-esteem and devours our self-confidence, causing us to feel hopeless.

Trust Him to be with you every step of the way. He will restore your hope. With God, those rivers of self-doubt become crossable and those mountains of fear become surmountable.

> He that dwelleth in the secret place of the most High shall abide under the shadow of the Almighty. I will say of the Lord, He is my refuge and my fortress: my God; in him will I trust. Surely he shall deliver thee from the snare of the fowler, and from the noisome pestilence. He shall cover thee with his feathers, and under his wings shalt thou trust: his truth shall be thy shield and buckler. (Psalm 91:1–4 KJV)

ABOUT THE SONG

I'm filled with gratitude for all the wonderful things God has allowed me to experience since I said yes to Him. None of this would be possible without Him. I don't know why I'm stricken with alopecia, but for whatever reason, God has allowed it to be so. I think of it like this: He trusts me. He trusts me to not give up. He trusts me to encourage others. He trusts me to give Him glory, because all that I have belongs to him.

Belongs To You

Verse 1
We lift our hands to the King of glory
We bow our knees before Your majesty
Exalted on the throne
Forever You will reign
There's no one like You
No one deserves our praise.

Chorus
It belongs to You
It belongs to You
All of our worship
Belongs to You.

Verse 2
You are the ruler of heaven and earth
We are amazed by Your wondrous works
Glorious is Your name
All nations will proclaim
There's no one greater
No one deserves our praise.

Bridge
Nobody else deserves it
There's no one greater.

CHAPTER 10

Permission to Shine

THE DAY I DECIDED TO LIVE my reality is my *reborn again day*. It's the day I made the choice to let God do whatever He wanted in my life. I embraced my bald head and accepted my identity in Christ. This is who I am, and through my journey, I know God will be glorified.

God has a purpose for each of us. From the foundation of the world, He called us and chose us for a specific assignment. We bring value to the kingdom, even with all our flaws, imperfections, insecurities, and inadequacies. We were chosen for a task that only we can do.

Your life experiences have operated as your on-the-job training to prepare you for the task. God can use every heartbreak, every disappointment, every unfortunate situation, every failure, and every discouraging word spoken against you for your good. "We know that all things work together for the good of those who love God—those whom he has called according to his plan" (Romans 8:28 GW). Now the question is, what is your purpose?

I believe nothing in our lives is an accident. We may not understand why certain things happened to us or even why we were given certain opportunities, like the time my parents paid for me to take piano lessons. I kicked and screamed and murmured and complained for six years until they were exhausted and gave in. Or the time when my father took me to musical theater auditions to help perfect my vocal ability, and I chose cheerleading instead. I didn't realize that God's purpose was to prepare me for what would come later. God uses our situations to prepare us for His purpose. It's never too late to find your God-given purpose. You may think you're too old to achieve a dream you had as a child. That is totally untrue. One of my favorite Scriptures speaks of bearing fruit in our mature years. Psalm 92 says,

> Yes! Look how you've made all your devoted lovers to flourish like palm trees, each one growing in victory, standing with strength! You've transplanted them into your heavenly courtyard, where they are thriving before you, for in your presence they will still overflow and be anointed. Even in their old age they will stay fresh, bearing luscious fruit and abiding faithfully. (Psalms 92:12–14 TPT)

Did you get it? The Bible declares "even in their old age" we will be fruitful. The world's standard tells us that as we mature, the window of opportunity to accomplish our dreams become narrower. I contend that we are never too old to fulfill our God-given purpose. Sarah was ninety years old when she gave birth to Isaac. It had been twenty-five years since God promised Abraham and Sarah that they would have a child—when she was still considered young, fertile, lively, and able to bear children. But twenty-five years later and no conception? I'm sure she was convinced it was done. Her childbearing years were over, but God had a plan for her.

The Enemy tries to abort God's plan for our lives, but God has not forgotten us. He has a plan designed just for each of us. I believe nothing in our life is an accident. We may not understand why certain things happened to us or even why we've had certain opportunities, but God does.

Sometimes we get stuck in our comfort zones that hinder us from walking in our purpose. Comfort zones are those places of neutrality, familiarity, and comfort that cause us to experience little to no anxiety. Comfort zones are risk-free and offer no incentives to stretch to new heights of performance. My aversion to coming out of my comfort zone has resulted in missed opportunities to stretch myself and grow. Even though I knew music was my passion and singing and playing made sense and would only enhance my abilities, I was afraid. I was afraid that I was not good enough, afraid of what others would think of my voice, and afraid that I would not measure up to others' expectations. I chose not to make that step out of my comfort zone because I was insecure and because it was too challenging. We will never grow if we don't face the hard things.

Comfort zones are like shadows. They are dark places in our lives that prevent us from shining. It could be a relationship that left you feeling inadequate or an injury that left you permanently scarred. Perhaps it was the years of verbal abuse that left you with a feeling of insecurity, or like me, it was the loss of hair resulting in a lost identity. Whatever your shadow, it causes your light to no longer shine bright. Shadows form when something or someone is blocking the light. Our comfort zone acts as a shelter, or a light blocker, to protect us from the negative thoughts and opinions of others.

God wants to be our shelter. Psalm 61:3 says, "For thou hast been a shelter for me, and a strong tower from the enemy" (KJV). There are times when we are our own worst enemy, making excuses to remain comfortable in the shadows. We often prefer to remain in dangerous environments, because leaving the familiar for the uncertain is unthinkable. What blocks us and keeps us from breaking free from our comfort zone? Could it be a lack of self-confidence? Or maybe it's fear of the unknown. It is frightening. It's like jumping off a cliff. The most fearful part of the journey is right before you take the plunge.

Comfort zones are like deserts. A desert is a place where there is little to no water. Where there is no water, there is no vegetation or growth. Because comfort zones do not push us to stretch ourselves and take on new challenges, we stop growing, becoming complacent and stagnant, like a body of water that breeds dangerous bacteria and parasites. Our minds begin to meditate on dangerous thoughts that sabotage our success. Thoughts of fear, inadequacies, defeat, loneliness, and pain all work against us, keeping us in bondage. The Bible instructs us to think on "things that are true, noble, right, pure, lovely, and honorable" (Philippians 4:8). It's time to leave our comfort zones and break free from the shadows.

There are some positives we gain from shadows. They suggest the presence of light. Light expels darkness, causing the darkness to disappear. An article in *Psychology Today*, "Gifts of the Shadow" by Julie Exline, suggests that not all shadows are bad: "Noticing the shadows may also draw our attention back to the light source that caused them." Jesus said, "I am the light of the world. Whoever follows me will not walk in darkness, but will have the light of life" (John 8:12 ESV). Not even the darkness of our comfort zones stands a chance against Jesus. He is the true light source. Consider inviting Jesus into your comfort zone so you can break free from the shadows.

When I allowed the true light source to illuminate the darkness in my mind, I began to walk in my purpose. I have been able to do things I never thought possible, like modeling. I didn't think I was pretty enough, tall enough, or thin enough to be a model—even when I had hair. I never imagined that with no hair, I'd walk a runway and shine for Him. I never thought it possible to write a book. I dropped out of my doctoral program for fear of writing my dissertation. Not only has God allowed me to write this book, but I am a collaborative author for *She Writes for Him: Black Voices of Wisdom*. He has given me songs to write and sing to inspire others to find their identity in Him, and He didn't stop there. I host a Facebook Live broadcast every Tuesday at 8 p.m. EST called *Onederfully Made*. It's designed to encourage listeners to love and embrace the person God created them to be, to be confident in their own skin, and to courageously embrace their imperfections. We all have them. Some happen to be more visible than others.

That's what it looks like to break out of the shadows and walk in the light of His glory. This is what He had planned for me all along, but my fears, insecurities, and poor self-esteem prevented me from living out His purpose and walking in His glory. God has so much more for us than we can ever think or imagine (Ephesians 3:20). I am not bragging about myself. I'm bragging about a gracious and loving God who values us and lavishes us with unfailing love. Scripture shows us just how generous God is.

> Everything we could ever need for life and godliness has already been deposited in us by his divine power. For all this was lavished upon us through the rich experience of knowing him who has called us by name and invited us to come to him through a glorious manifestation of his goodness. (2 Peter 3:4 TPT)

Can you see God's goodness? Did you hear your name? He called us by name. He has already given it to us. It's been deposited in our lives. Now it's up to us to believe it, take ownership of it, and claim it as ours. What God has done for me, He can also do for you. Not only can He do it, but He wants to do it. He wants to take you from bondage to freedom, from defeat to victory, and from humiliation to honor.

I've learned some valuable lessons along my journey. First, we are not defined by our outward appearance as society leads us to believe. Images we see on television and social media sometimes perpetuate a fraud. People go to great lengths to cover up exterior flaws and imperfections, but inwardly their hearts are weary and wounded.

I am not that little girl putting yarn on my head pretending to have long hair anymore. I learned I am not my hair or the lack of it. I am who God says I am.

Second, we are not defined by the indelible scars stamped on our souls as a result of bullying and name calling, isolation and exclusion, emotional and sexual abuse, or rape and molestation. I'm no longer the little girl left on the sideline. I'm in the game. We cannot change our past, but we don't have to allow these experiences to control our future, destroy us, and rob us of our purpose. God sent His Son to give us abundant life (John 10:10). Live that abundant life.

I am no longer that young woman who crumbled under embarrassment and retreated into a cocoon when called bald-headed. I am a beautiful butterfly who represents hope, change, and freedom.

I have also learned that the pursuit of superficial things only brings us into bondage. God desires for us to be free—free to be who He made us to be. Galatians 5:1 (TPT) says, "At last we have freedom, for Christ has set us free! We must always cherish this truth and firmly refuse to go back into the bondage of our past." I was a slave to my wig as I hid in the shadows. Now I choose to boldly live my reality out loud and let God's light shine fully through me.

God gives us permission to shine for Him. It's time to turn up the flicker and shine brightly and unapologetically. Maybe situations and circumstances, sometimes out of our control, caused your light to dim. Perhaps an abusive relationship dulled your glow, or maybe not winning the beauty contest attacked your self-esteem, and now you only have a twinkle. Whatever the reasons, we retreat into shadows God never intended for us. God wants us to come out of those places of comfort, those stagnant places, so He can receive the glory of His beautiful creation.

Challenge yourself by moving toward your fears. Stretch yourself by trying something new. Grow yourself by starting conversations with strangers. Join a support group. Switch up your routines. Date yourself. Treat yourself. Love yourself. Embrace the person God created you to be, and shine. There is a song of unknown origin that says, "This little light of mine, I'm gonna let it shine." Shine because God gave you His light. When I taught at a Christian school, the students and I especially loved singing the next verse of the song. "Hide it under a bushel, no (emphatically), I'm gonna let it shine." No more hiding in shadows. No more dwelling in comfort zones. Jesus said, "Ye are the light of the world. A city that is set on an hill cannot be hid" (Matthew 5:14 KJV). *The Message* translation put it this way: "You're here to be light, bringing out the God-colors in the world." The God-colors are you and the amazing God-given gift and purpose for your life.

Now it's your time to shine, to break free from the bondage, and to walk out from the shadows and into the light of His glory. I realize that people who suffer with alopecia may choose to continue to wear wigs, and that's okay. My journey to finding freedom and rest in God may look different from yours. But whatever your struggles and challenges—domestic violence, child abuse, abandonment, cancer, depression, addiction—they do not define you. You are a light, so be determined to shine for His glory. As the children's song says, "Let it shine; let it shine; let it shine."

> Let your light so shine before men, that they may see your good works and glorify your Father in heaven. (Matthew 5:16 KJV)

ABOUT THIS SONG

I cowrote this song with my friend Jacki Waller Barineau. It is a powerful reminder of the resurrection of Christ. Not only did He set us free from the power of sin but also from all our fears, doubts, depression, broken hearts, and sicknesses. They are "gone, gone, gone—all rolled away."

Rolled Away

Verse 1
In the darkness of the night
They led my Savior away
All hope was gone, His time had come
His closest friends betrayed
He died a criminal's death
They thought it was the end
They never realized
This all was in God's plan.

Pre-Chorus
The earth quaked, the rocks split
Graves were opened, the veil was ripped
And when morning came on that third day
Night was gone, life had won!

Chorus
The stone was rolled away
He came back to life, walked out of the grave
My past was washed away
All because of the day
The stone was rolled away.

Verse 2
In the dark times of our lives
Overtaken with every chain

It can seem all hope is gone
Full of shame, full of pain.
But Jesus has set us free
Death has lost its sting
And the morning brings new life
We have the victory.

Bridge

Leader: Fear, doubt, sin, all rolled away
Congregation: Gone, gone, gone, all rolled away
Leader: Depression, loneliness, pain, all rolled away
Congregation: Gone, gone, gone, all rolled away.

Leader: Sickness, disease, broken hearts, all rolled away
Congregation: Gone, gone, gone, all rolled away
Leader: Weakness, death, defeat, all rolled away
Congregation: Gone, gone, gone, all rolled away.

Leader: Strongholds, oppression, captivity, all rolled away
Congregation: Gone, gone, gone, all rolled away
Leader: Addictions, afflictions, insecurity, all rolled away
Congregation: Gone, gone, gone, all rolled away.

Leader: Worry, confusion, stress, all rolled away
Congregation: Gone, gone, gone, all rolled away
Leader: Guilt, shame, my past . . .
Congregation: Gone, gone . . .

Acknowledgments

Thank you to my wonderful husband, Kim, for never giving up on us. You stuck with me through the good, the bad, and the bald. God could not have given me a better partner. I love doing life with you. You are the real Superman.

To my awesome son, Kimmel, you are gifted beyond what you imagine. I am inspired by your ability to master any instrument you touch. Don't give up on your dreams. There is greatness in you. You are the real Superstar.

To my amazing daughter, Kimmaya, you have made me so proud. Thank you for always supporting me in all my endeavors and encouraging me to be myself. You have inspired me more than you'll ever know. Thank you for always having my back. You are my real Ride or Die.

To my beloved father, the late Rev. Dr. Eric A. Mayes, Jr., thank you for being a trailblazer and leaving such a great legacy. You saw greatness in me, and I'm striving every day to make you proud. I only pray I can continue your legacy for my children. You are the real MVP.

To my beautiful mother, Mrs. Bernice Mayes, you are the epitome of beauty and grace inside and out. Even though Alzheimer's has robbed you, I know you are there fighting to return, responding to my voice every time I sing to you. You are the real Champion.

Thank you to the best siblings in the universe. Joyce, Shirley, Eric III, Floyd, and Kay, you have been Team Fe my entire life. You pushed me even when I didn't want to be pushed. You are the real Cheer Squad.

Thank you to Athena Dean Holtz and the amazing staff at Redemption Press for believing in me and taking me from novice to a published author. You are the real Dream Team.

Above all, I thank God for His architectural design and purpose for my life; for Jesus, who made the fulfillment of the purpose possible through salvation; and for the Holy Spirit, who guides me in carrying the purpose to completion. Working together, they are my true inspiration.

Resources

1. Davis, E. *Graffiti*. Chicago: Moody Publishers. 2008.
2. Edwards, J. "Undetected Spiritual Pride: One Cause of Failure in Times of Great Revival," http://www.grace-abounding.com/Articles/Sin/Pride_Edwards.htm.
3. Exline, J. "Gifts of the Shadow" *Psychology Today*, February 1, 2013. https://www.psychologytoday.com/us/blog/light-and-shadow/201302/gifts-the-shadow.
4. Gilbert, Paul. *The Compassionate Mind: A New Approach to Life's Challenges*. Oakland, CA: New Harbinger Publications. 2010.
5. "Hair Loss in Women." WebMD Medical Reference from the American Hair Loss Association. 2010. https://www.webmd.com/skin-problems-and-treatments/hair-loss/hair-loss-medref.
6. Hungerford, M. W. *Molly Bawn*. London: Smith, Elder, & Co. 1878.
7. Othman, Noor Ahnis, Noor Rahmat, Mohd Kasim, and Aini Akmar. "The Cycle of Self-fulfilling Prophecy in Academic Writing. European Journal of Education Studies." Volume 5, Issue 11, 2019. https://oapub.org/edu/index.php/ejes/article/view/2326/4965.
8. Popkin, S. *Comparison Girl*. Grand Rapids, MI: Kregel Publications. 2020.
9. Vine, W. E., Unger, M. F., White, W., & Vine, W. E. (1985). Vine's complete expository dictionary of Old and New Testament words. Nashville: Nelson.
10. www.dictionary.com.

ORDER INFORMATION

To order additional copies of this book, please visit
www.redemption-press.com.
Also available on Amazon.com and BarnesandNoble.com
or by calling toll-free 1-844-2REDEEM.
To download digital copies of Carol's music on Spotify or
Apple Music,
scan the QR codes below:

CPSIA information can be obtained
at www.ICGtesting.com
Printed in the USA
JSHW022043260523
42215JS00004B/29

9 781646 453061